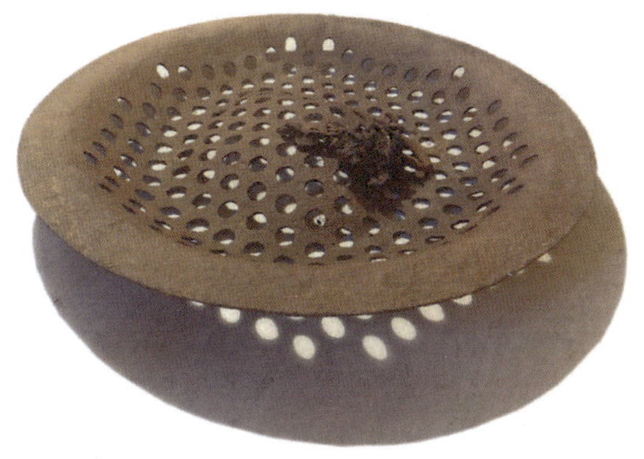

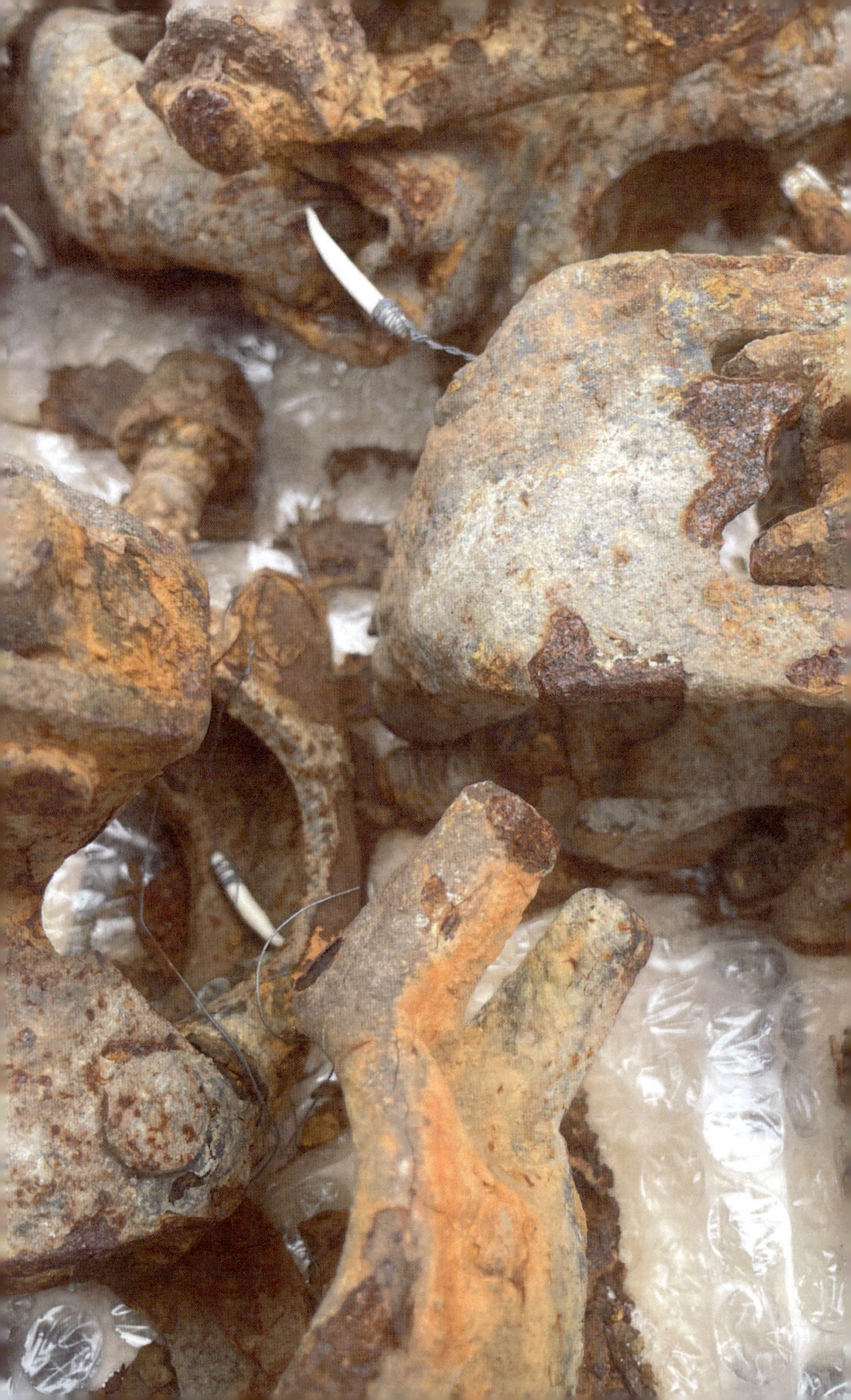

The Camden Town Hoard

A collection of archeological artefacts
excavated along London's Regent's Canal
during summer 2021

Curated and introduced by

Natalia Zagórska-Thomas

Foreword by

David Thorp

On Expurgamento *by*

Christopher Reid

Contributors (in order of appearance)

Róisín Tierney, Simon Zagórski-Thomas, Kevin Boniface,
Ian Duhig, Alex Zagórska-Thomas, Adam Stinson, Nancy
Campbell, Julian Stannard, Phyllis Stein, Marius Kociejowski,
Katy Evans-Bush, Will Eaves, Amy McCauley, Gavin Clarke,
Charles Boyle, Natalia Zagórska-Thomas, Ruth Fainlight,
Mervyn Diese, Sophie Herxheimer, Helen Wilks, Christopher
Reid, Andrzej Maria Borkowski

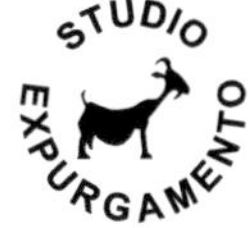

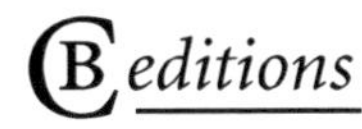

First published in 2022
by Studio Expurgamento
132D Camden Street London NW1 0HY
www.studioexpurgamento.com

with CB editions
146 Percy Road
London W12 9QL
www.cbeditions.com

Printed in England by Mixam, Hertfordshire

ISBN 978-0-9955057-1-1

Foreword by David Thorp

A (very) brief history of scavenging and theft

I have no doubt I shall, please Heaven, begin to be more
beforehand with the world, and to live in a perfectly new
manner if – if, in short, anything turns up.
– Mr Micawber in Charles Dickens, *David Copperfield*

In the heyday of museum growth in the late 1890s
each museum had its keeper whose job was to keep
the building and the things it housed in good repair.
The keeper was the custodian of the museum and
the curator of its collection. But the purpose of the
museum has changed. As has that of the curator, the
exhibition, the artefact, and the audience. Now we are
all curators, organising and exhibiting our lives.

As we await the coronation of King Charles III, some
fuss has been made about whether the crown of the
old Queen Elizabeth the Queen Mother should adorn
the head of Camilla, the new Queen Consort. This is
because sitting atop the crown is one of the largest
cut diamonds in the world, the Koh-I-Noor. How did it
get up there? Largely as the result of a lot of fighting
between a very assorted bunch of men over a long
period of time. So much so that it is now said to bring
bad luck to any man who wears it and is reserved solely
for the adornment of women. Normally tucked away in
the Tower of London among the Crown Jewels, given its
history, booty of the British Empire, its flawed brilliance
will probably not be seen in public ceremony again.
Put alongside the Elgin Marbles, the Benin Bronzes
and countless other contested artefacts as well as all
those little souvenirs in the homes of the middle-class
administrators of the British empire, the memento mori
of the days of Kenya's Happy Valley, the Raj and all the

rest, it makes for quite a haul. To quote Yasmin Alibhai
-Brown (*The i*, 31 August 2020)., 'Our museums are full
of stolen colonial loot.'

Back in the 18th and 19th centuries mudlarks
scavenged in the mud on the banks of the River Thames
for anything that could be sold. Their description in
Wikipedia is chastening reading: 'Becoming a mudlark
was usually a choice dictated by poverty and lack of
skills. Work conditions were filthy and uncomfortable, as
excrement and waste would wash onto the shores from
the raw sewage as well as the corpses of humans, cats
and dogs.'

And so to art and James Joyce who, during a
visit to Austria in 1929, discovered Adolph Johannes
Fischer's *Fluviana*, photographs of curiously formed
tree roots that he then appropriated and published in

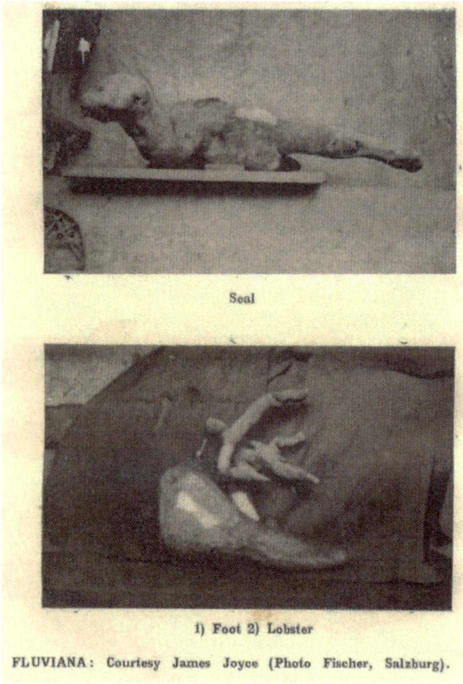

Fluviana: page from *transition*, 1929

the avant-garde magazine *transition*. The objects had already been given titles according to the shapes they suggested: 'Hydra', 'Foot', 'Lobster', 'Head of Gazelle' and so on. Joyce adopted or modified the titles of these objects, appropriating the images in an act similar to that of many of today's conceptual artists.

In 1999 the American artist Mark Dion and a team of helpers combed the banks of the Thames near Tate Modern. They unearthed a wide variety of artefacts relating to the history of the river and of London. Working in less chastening conditions than their erstwhile counterparts, the finds of these modern-day mudlarks included clay pipes, animal bones, earthenware and plastic toys that were then cleaned and classified by a team of local volunteers. These treasures are now beautifully catalogued and housed in the Tate collection in fine vitrines with the added value that the art market bestows; an artwork by Dion can be valued at anything between £3,000 and £50,000.

More recently, during lockdown, in order to remedy a potential public hazard a public-spirited citizen with a barge and the necessary wherewithal has been dredging the Regents Canal in Camden, dumping piles of muddy waste on its banks. Another artist-curator, **Natalia Zagórska-Thomas**, fascinated by what might turn up, has been filtering through these heaps of detritus, discovering and revealing the riches of what has become The Camden Town Hoard: the subject of this book.

David Thorp is a veteran curator who also practises as an artist using his birth name Jeffrey Bligh.

Introduction

An object exists between the rubbish heap and eternity.
– Tadeusz Kantor

I feel an affinity for art when it is a form of existence, like when shamans worked in the territory between men and unknown powers. – Magdalena Abakanowicz

The Camden Town Hoard is a collection of archaeological finds dredged up from a section of Regent's Canal, roughly between Granary Square in Kings Cross and the London Zoo.

The canal was dredged by an unknown person in the spring/summer of 2021 during lockdown. The majority of the objects revealed during this time were removed from the canal towpaths by Camden Council but not before 20 or so most fascinating artefacts were rescued and accessioned into the ExPurgamento archive.

Since then the collection has been studied, thoroughly documented and provided with museum labels by a team of highly trained experts from a broad variety of backgrounds and interests. What is rather unusual for a grouping of archaeological objects found together in a specific location is that they seem to represent various historical periods and geographical locations both real and imagined.

This intriguing find attracted attention of several august institutions, most notably the Institute for the Study of Found Objects of a Perplexing Nature, the Dubious Context Society and the Notional Heritage Trust, thanks to whose generous support the study into the collection can continue, and further excavations are planned in the near future.

Identifying and contextualising the various objects belonging to the Camden Town Hoard threw up several new problems related to taxonomical classification. Specifically, it has been noted that the term 'artefact' may not be an entirely sufficient or appropriate description of all archaeological material and it is therefore proposed that the term 'artefiction' might sometimes be used instead.

The Camden Town Hoard was exhibited at St John's Church, Waterloo, as part of the London Group's summer exhibition during Waterloo Festival in 2021. It is hoped that the growing collection will be able to tour the country in the forthcoming years as the crucial and rigorous work of putting it in the wider context of British cultural heritage continues.

Natalia Zagórska-Thomas
Curator, Studio ExPurgamento

With grateful thanks to:
The Institute for the Study of Found Objects of
a Perplexing Nature
The Dubious Context Society
The Notional Heritage Trust
The London Group
The Camden Town Hoard Expert Panel

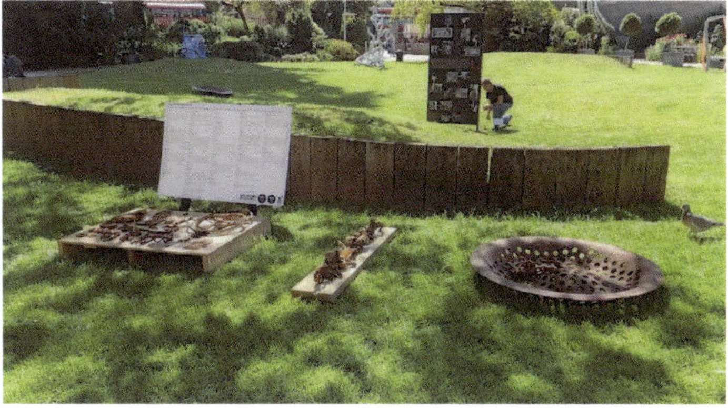
The Camden Town Hoard at St John's Church, Waterloo, 2021

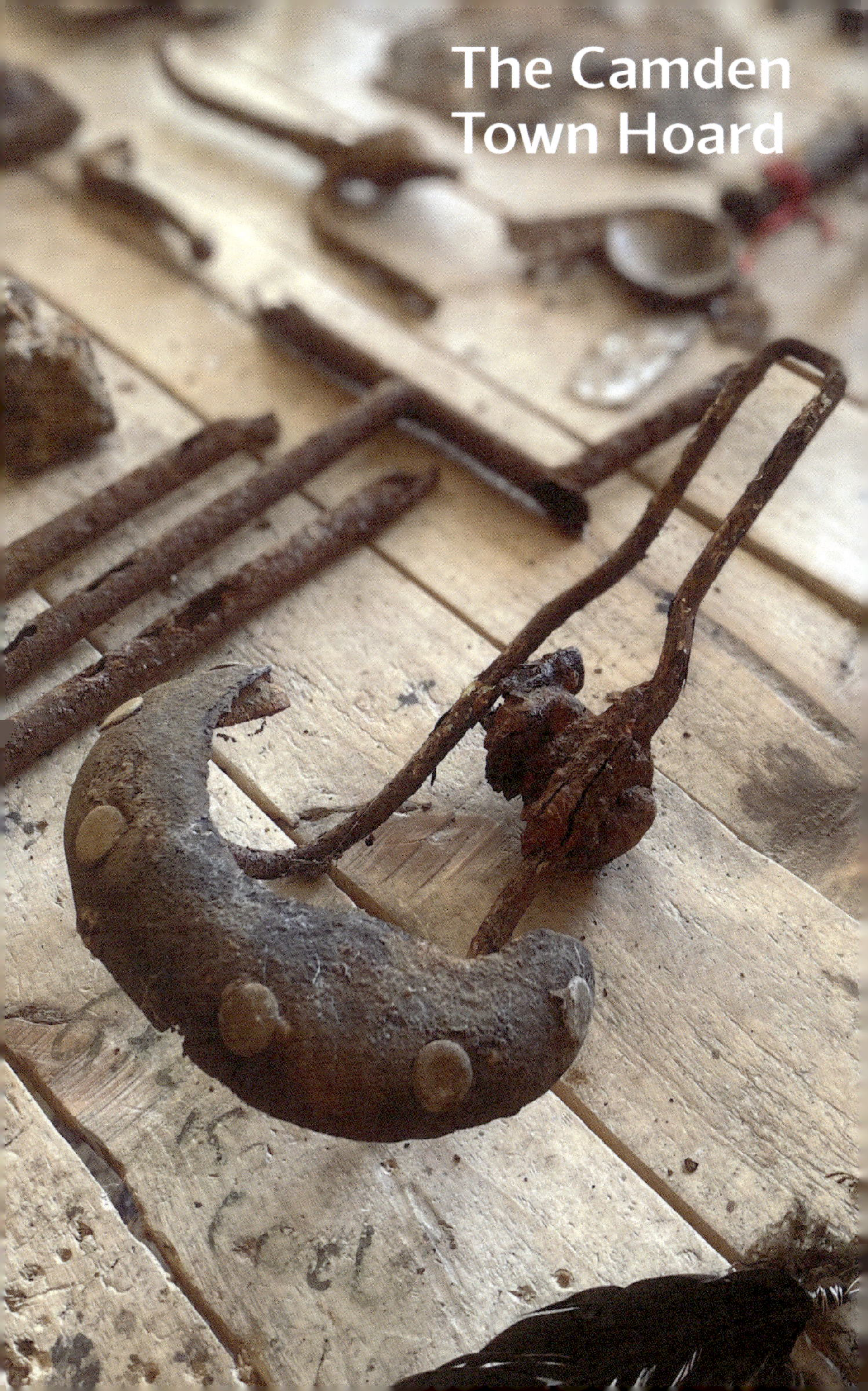
The Camden
Town Hoard

Toothpick of a giantess

Iron, North-Eastern Siberia, 800 BCE

Thrown up by the melting permafrost, and at first
thought to be the cloak-pin of a high-ranking,
possibly royal, member of an early nomadic tribe.
Closer examination has revealed it to be a toothpick,
its grooves and markings caused by very large,
female, humanoid teeth. Carbon dating places it in
the Early European Iron Age. Minute traces of DNA
reveal the owner's likely diet: berries, nuts, reindeer
meat, small children.

No. 1123/51
2021.3-19   Róisín Tierney

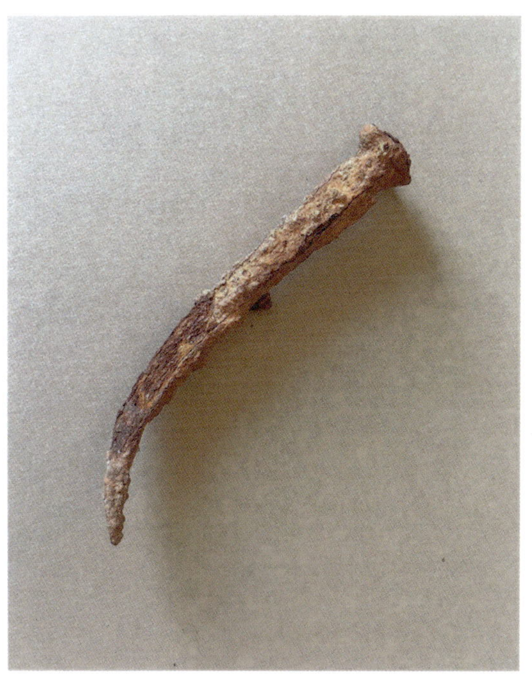

The Godgifu Breastplate

Iron and glass, early 7th century

Found during the 1973 renovation of the Unruly Goat
pub in Bromeswell, Suffolk, not far from Sutton Hoo,
this fragment of armour dates from King Rædwald's
reign during the Wuffingas dynasty, Kingdom of East
Anglia. The armour belonged to Godgifu (latinised as
Godiva), the daughter of Hroðgar (latinised as *Roger*),
a *median thegn* – a middle-ranking nobleman – who
died around 615 BCE. The amber glass 'breast' is most
likely a fragment of a late Roman/Byzantine drinking
vessel, later incorporated into the armour. The
small, circular holes in the stomacher were settings
for a collection of silver/*niello* circular brooches
common to the period. Godgifu owned a highly
prized collection of these brooches depicting seven
pagan deities including Woden, þunor, Tiw, and Frig.
According to one Anglo-Saxon chronicle Godgifu was
murdered by Æbbe, the daughter of a rival *thegn*, who
stabbed her with a *seax* or dagger before prising the
brooches from her breastplate. The fate of Æbbe or
the stolen brooch collection is unknown.

No. 1123/36
2021.3-10   Simon Zagórski-Thomas

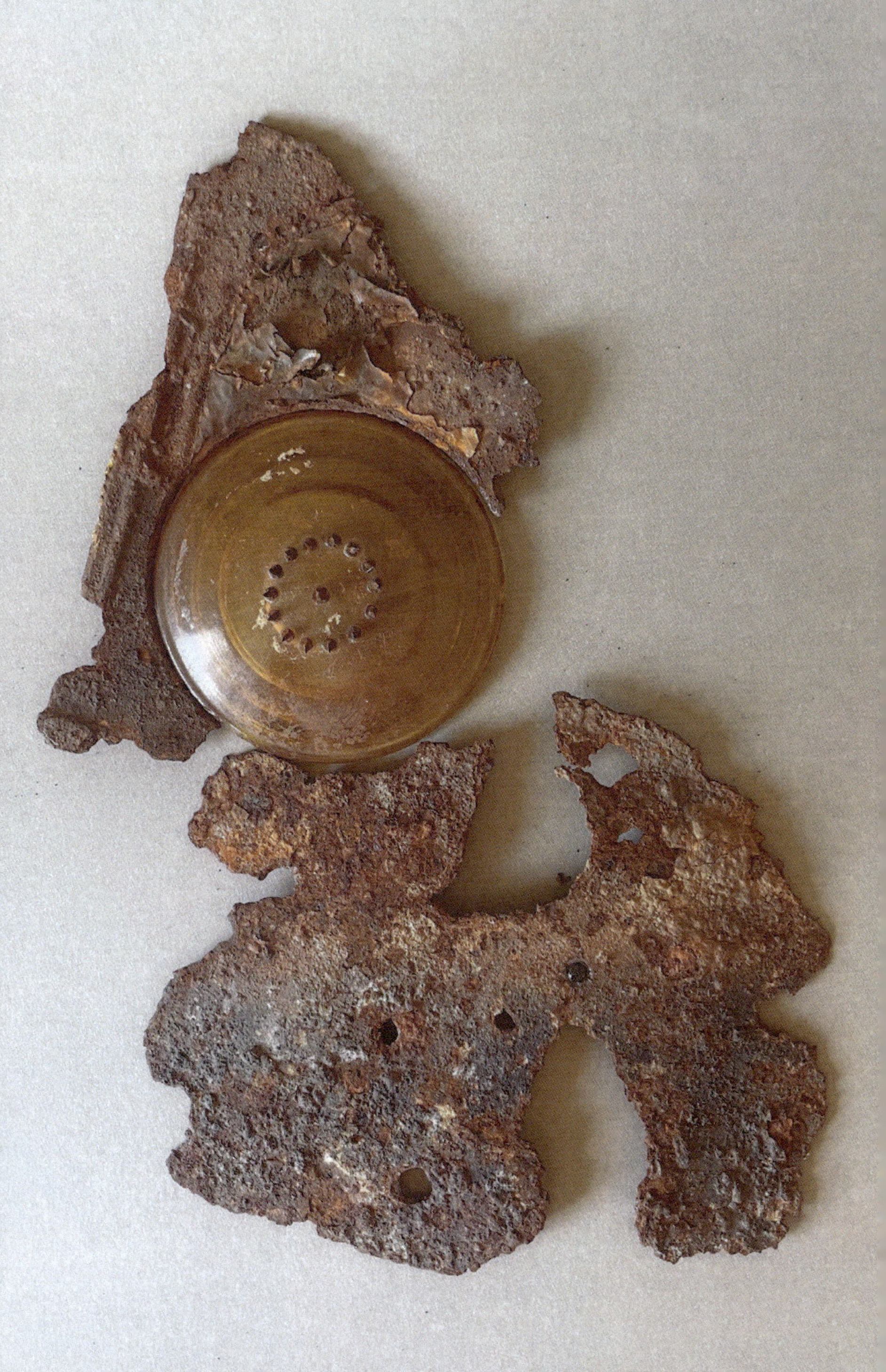

A Boggard's Sneck

Lid and stopper from a traditional weeting pot, 17th century

The ignorance of many in the 17th century meant
that belief in superstition was rife and ordinary
mishaps were often attributed to 'boggards'
(malevolent *genii locorum*). When a member of a
household fell ill, the boggard was invariably blamed
and a 'weeting pot' would be filled with 'watter' (urine
and strong alcohol) and placed in the chimney breast
overnight. The boggard would not be able to resist
the watter and would enter the weeting pot via the
chimney flue, imbibe from it, and fall asleep inside. In
the morning the boggard's sneck would be used to
secure the boggard who would only be released once
the ill person had recovered their health.

No. 1123/52
2021.3-18

Kevin Boniface

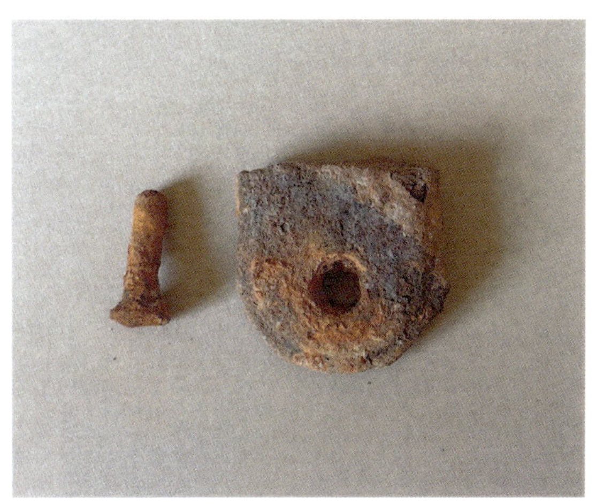

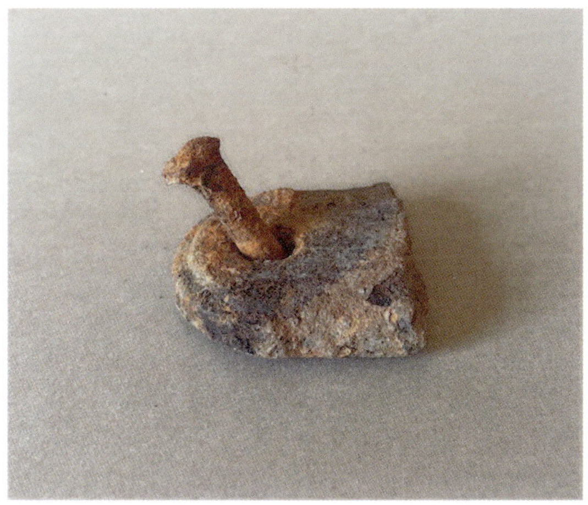

Akimbo Strut

When the 'akimbo' stance for signalling exasperation
became widely used by parents, teachers, policemen
and trainers of military personnel during the early
Edwardian period, it was found to be an exhausting
position to maintain for extended lengths of time
if unusually difficult charges required it. Thus the
invention of the 'akimbo strut' by Jeremiah Wison
was particularly helpful, which could be secreted in
'leg-of-mutton' blouse-sleeves and under military
capes or academic gowns, enabling the wearer to
keep their infuriated posture almost indefinitely.
Normally, Wilson's struts were made from wood,
but for especially stupid or recalcitrant groups they
could be cast in metal, as with this exhibit, which was
retrieved from the crook in an elbow of a skeleton
found at the bottom of the Regent's Canal. That the
top of the cranium of this skeleton had apparently
blown outward, with fragments of an old mortar
board attached to the ragged hole, has led some
archaeologists to speculate that the remains belonged
to a local teacher, so long ignored or mocked by their
pupils that for all their akimbo-strut reinforcement
their head eventually exploded with frustration. The
pupils, in this theory, stricken with fear, or perhaps
guilt, tossed their teacher's body with the akimbo
strut still strapped in place to weigh it down into the
murky waters of the nearby canal to disguise what had
happened. Successfully, it would seem.

No. 1123/17
2021.3-03   Ian Duhig

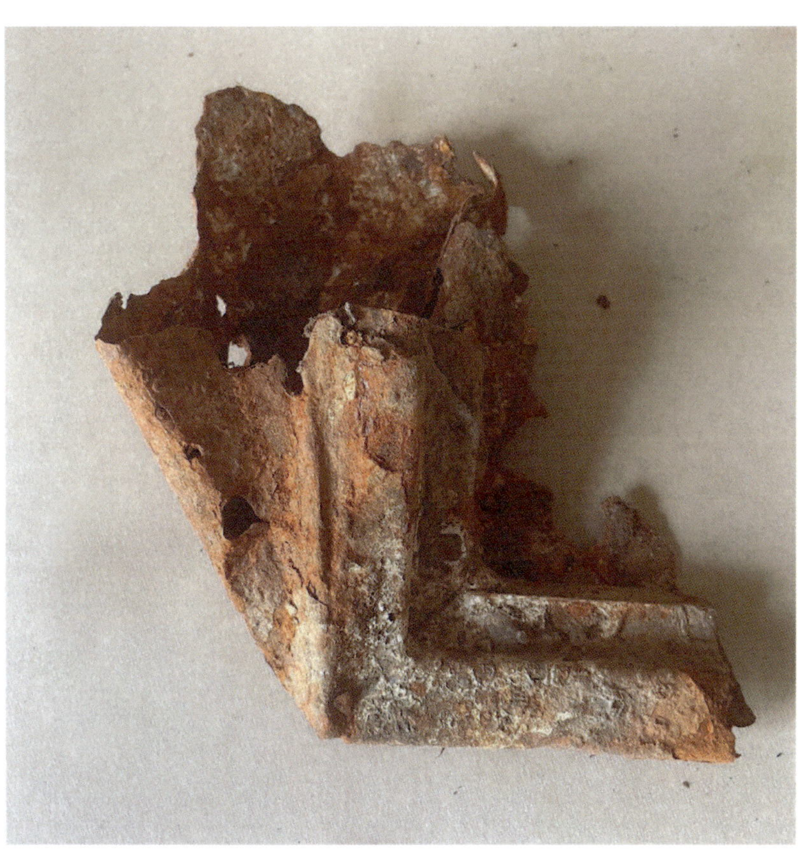

Scooby
Steel coated tungsten,* 1941

Diving weight for a small to medium-sized dog.

* Tungsten, or wolfram, is a chemical element with the symbol W
and atomic number 74. Tungsten is a rare metal found naturally
on Earth almost exclusively as compounds with other elements.
It was identified as a new element in 1781 and first isolated as a
metal in 1783.

No. 1123/55
2021.3-04   Alexandra Zagórska-Thomas / Adam Stinson

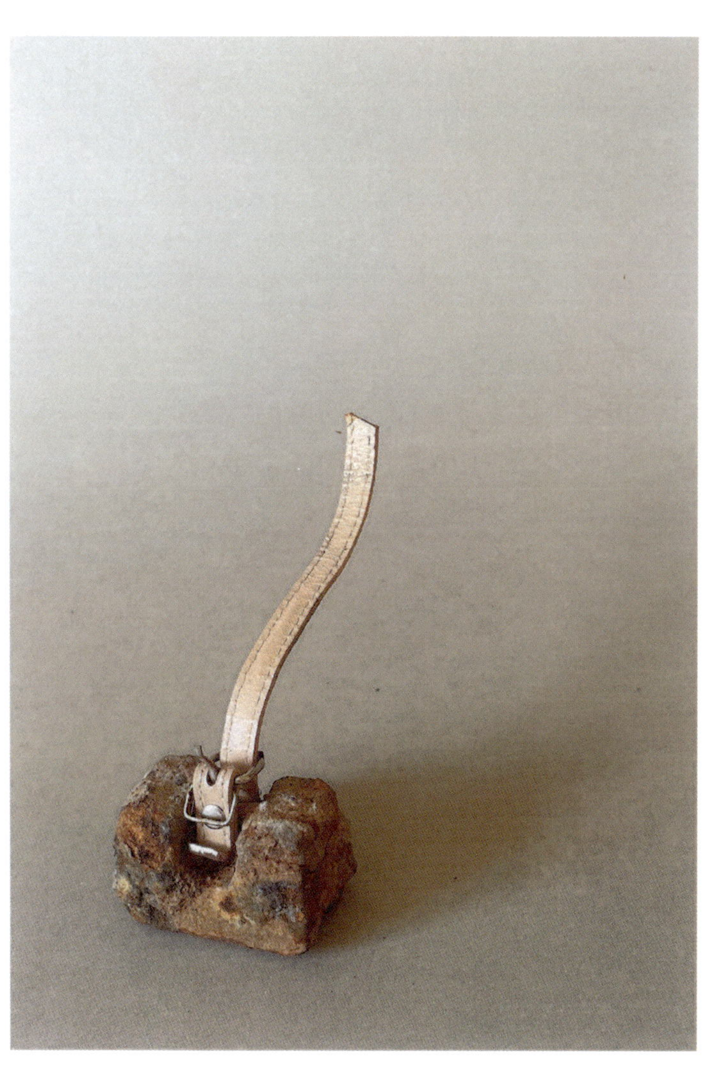

Paradox ladder

Unknown metal, 4th millennium

A single, central handrail and rare open-rung structure
characterise this apparatus, designed by one-armed
post-human beings to scale regions of spacetime with
strong gravitational fields such as black holes. Clearly
a fragment of a far longer span, Zvegintzov (2019)
surmises its irruption though a wormhole to 20th-
century Camden Town while being employed to move
through, and measure, the singularity at the heart
of Sagittarius A*. Named after the *twin paradox*, a
thought experiment in Special Relativity, in which a
person who makes a journey into space at high speed
will return home to find they have aged less than an
identical twin who stayed on Earth.

No. 1123/60

2021.3-14

Nancy Campbell

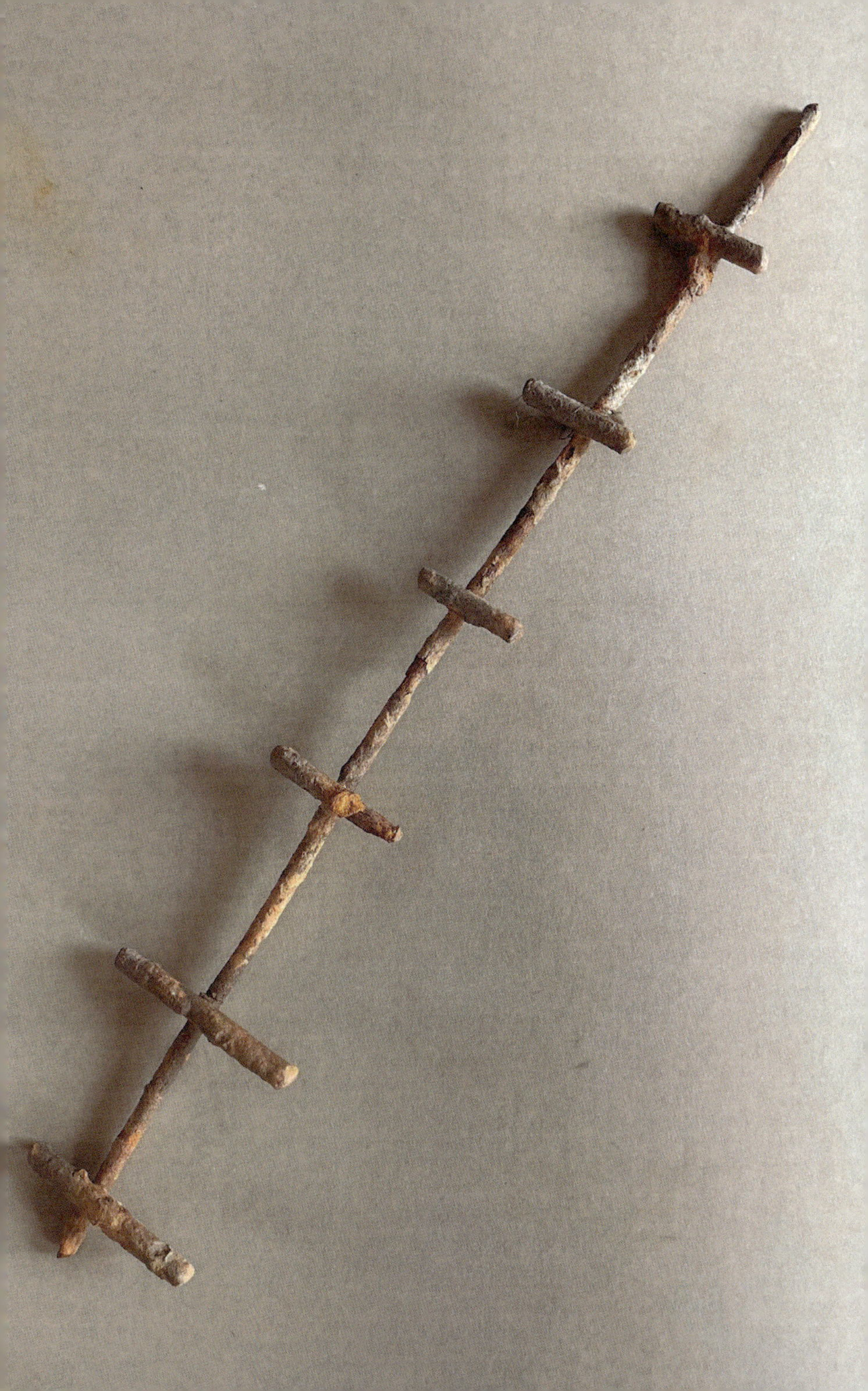

Knife fetish

Iron, wood, date unknown

It's post-neanderthal, it's something.
Even in the past there was boredom.
No fighting, no hunting and
the children restless so the Headman
gathers his people and holds up
the fetish someone found in the lake.
All eyes look at it, he waves it around.

No. 1123/48
2021.3-09   Julian Stannard

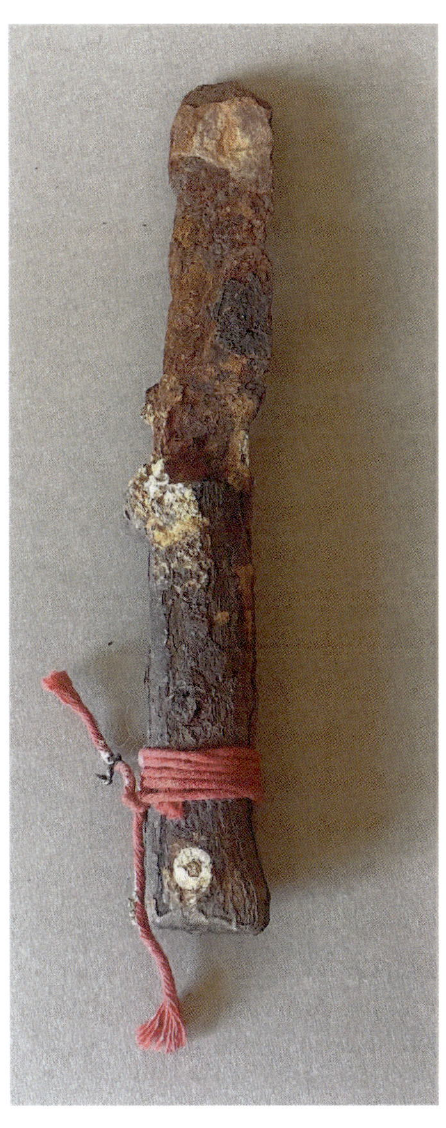

Lulapeg

Fragment, c.970

The lulapeg was an accordion-like instrument played by itinerant street musicians. In *De Rerum Popularis*, a 12th-century treatise on popular culture, Gilbert of Harlesden claimed that in the hands of a gifted player the metal keys of the lulapeg were endowed with a capacity to change their physical state, folding and unfolding according to the emotional contours of the music.

No. 1123/46
2021.3-27

Phyllis Stein

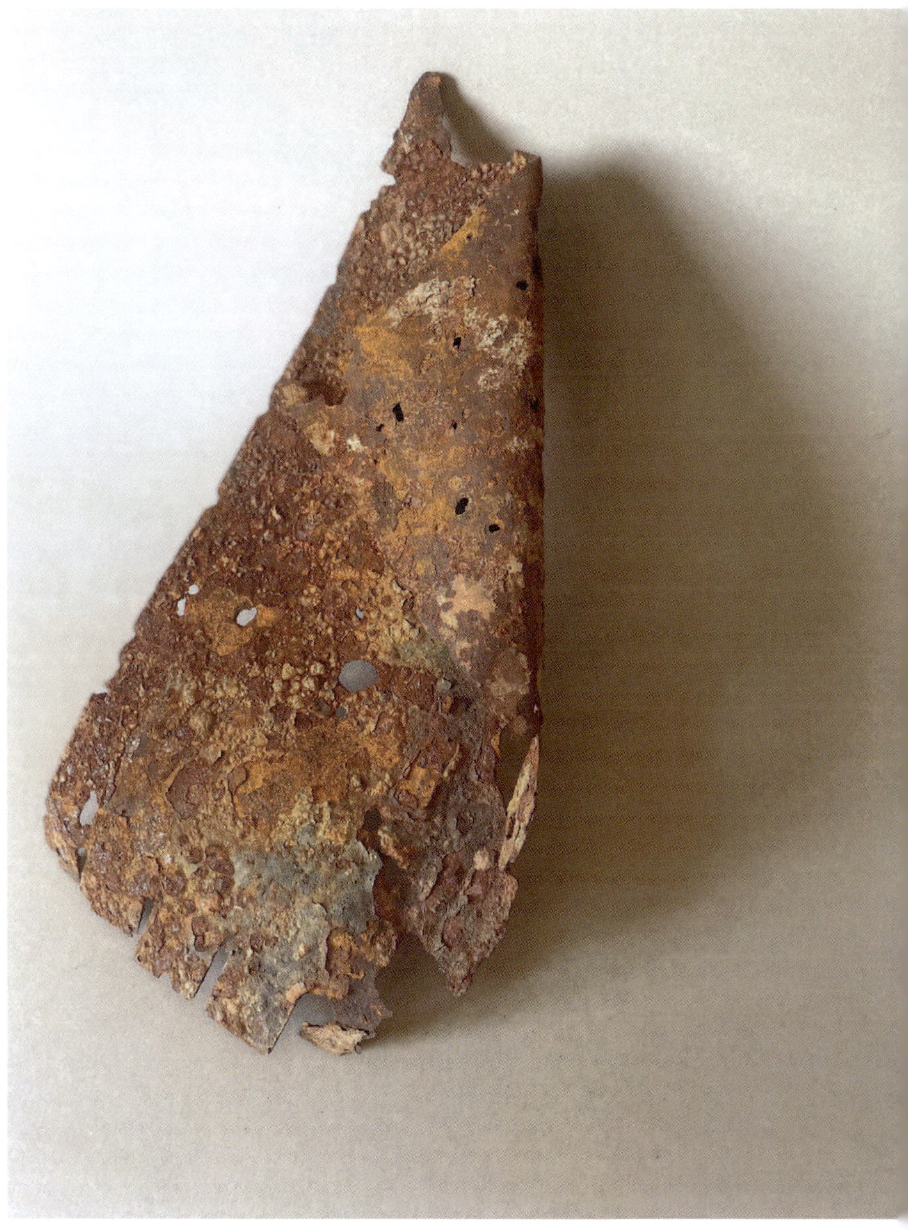

Iron Age medical instrument
Approx. 800–950 BCE

The circular part of the instrument was used to isolate
a tonsular cyst which was then held in place with one
hand while with the other the surgeon (or shaman)
cut away the cyst. It would be another three millennia
before antibiotics came into use, and so the rate of
infection was probably high with resultant deaths. The
cysts were themselves often a consequence of failed
primitive tonsillectomies. Yarrow (*Achillea millefolium*),
traces of which can be seen just below the circular
area, was applied as an astringent to reduce bleeding.
As there was little knowledge about how the body
works, ailments were put down to supernatural causes,
often evil spirits. Its discovery has led to speculation
that Camden Town was once the site of an Iron Age
hill fort.

No. 1123/61
2021.3-14b   Marius Kociejowski

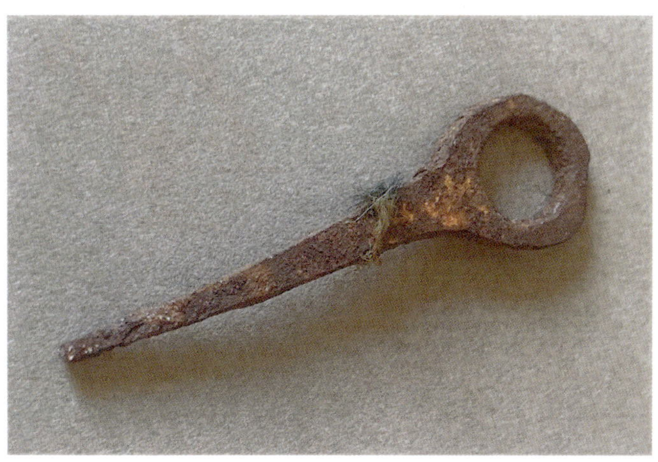

Rhetorical Device

Early Iron Age

With the development of farming came notions of property and land ownership. Disputes were more frequent before the invention of chainlink fencing.

Most people were unable to read, though language itself was in a very rich, complex phase of its development, and arguments would spring from nowhere, often over something very small, like a chicken (*Gallus gallus domesticas* [*Phasianidae*]).

Little is known about this device, except that it cuts both ways. It was worn on the wrist.

In a period known for tools, and increasingly sophisticated swords and other weapons, the bluntness of this small instrument is remarkable.

Scholars are unsure whether it was a tempering device for the argumentative and overbearing, or a mark of wisdom, but it remains an innovative early use of external objects in the human quest for clear thinking.

It does not appear in literature, hence there is no known name for it. But a pictogram including an early Rhetorical Device and shouting man (not a nobleman) has been identified in a tiny fragment of a much earlier draft of *Gilgamesh*, indicating that the culture had high aspirations for social activity. History shows that, like all others, these fell short of the ideal.

No. 1123/56

2021.3-23

Katy Evans-Bush

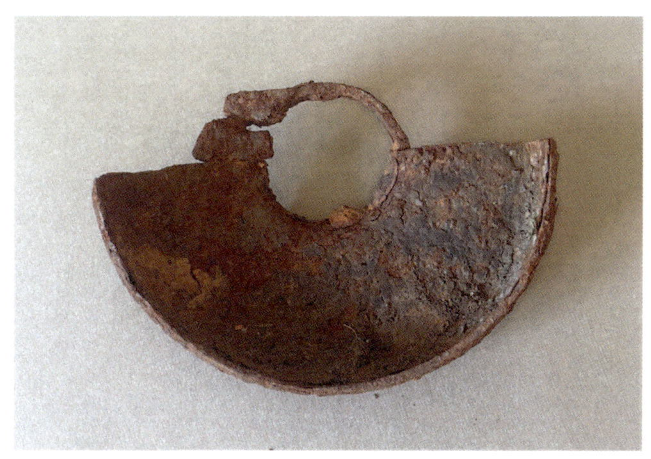

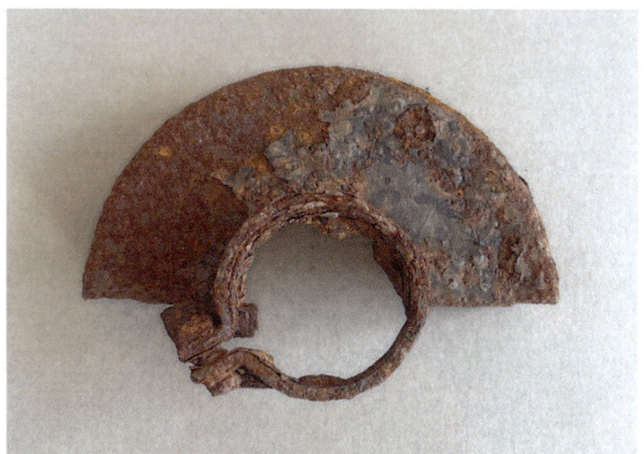

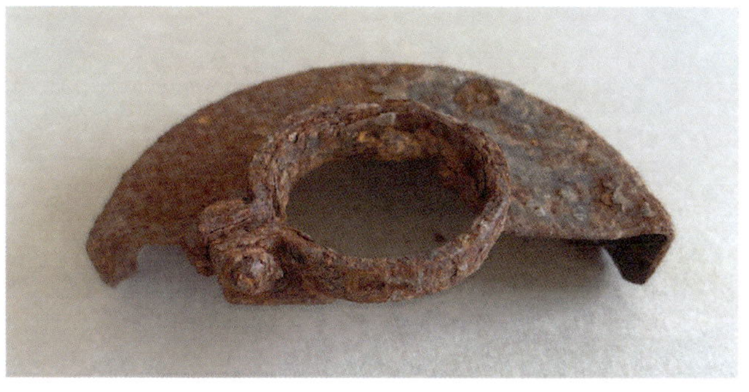

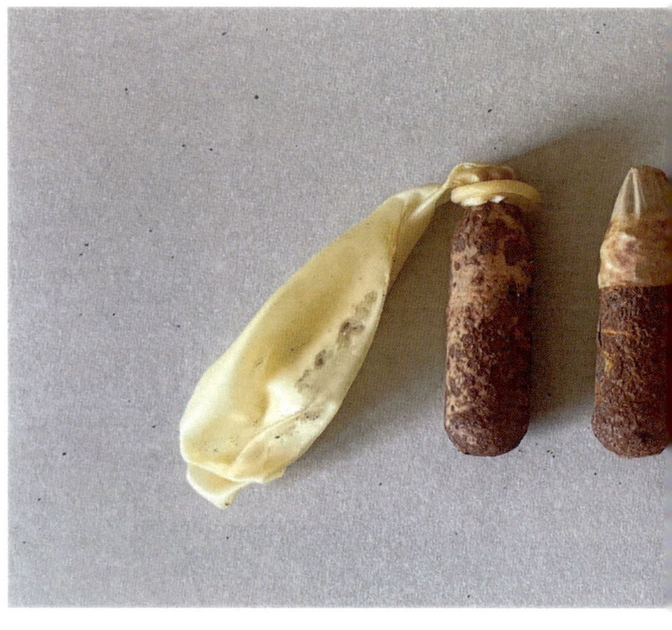

Rat aqualung

Netherlands, 1973?

These cylinders formed part of a veterinary
programme initiated by the Dutch zoologist
Miriam Hoeghege at the University of Utrecht
in 1971. Hoeghege was studying the effects
of habitat fragmentation on aquatic wildlife
in the Amstel when she established the link
between pollution-driven immunosuppression
and respiratory disease in riverine mammals,
especially water voles. Take-up was encouraging
among voles and cognate species, who adapted

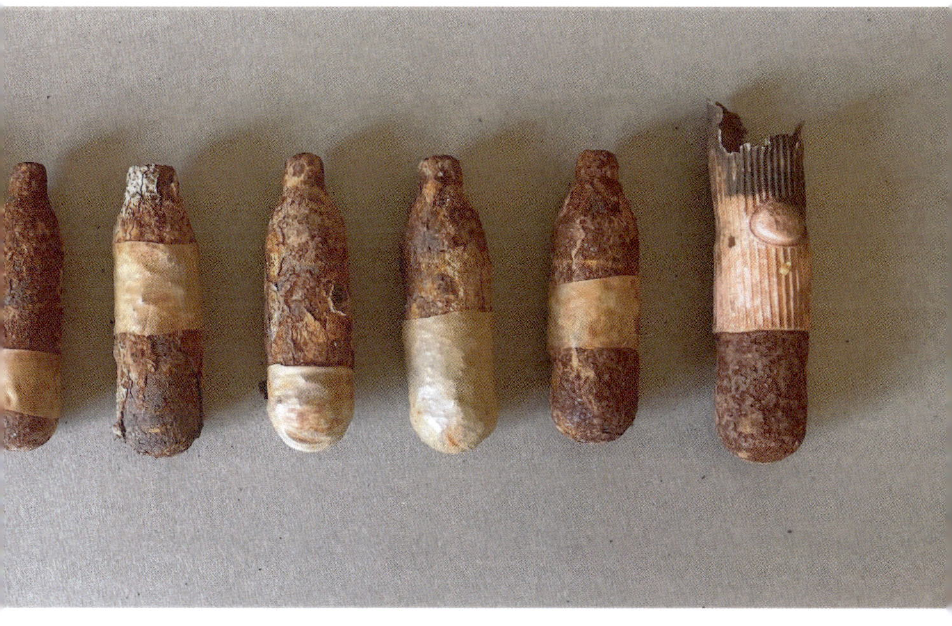

easily to the breathing apparatus and recovered pulmonary function in most cases. The compressed-air cylinders in this image date from the infamous and explosive second stage of the programme, after *Waterschap Amstel, Gooi en Vecht* withdrew its funding.

On loan from the Museum van Onopzettelijke Wreedheid

No. 1123/33

2021.3-27

Will Eaves

Wedding dance ring

Origin: Terenure, Dublin, *c.*200 BCE

A well-preserved example of the 'gerrup' or shared
dance ring. Example of the marriage goods of the
Parisi tribe from Yorkshire discovered in Ireland and
thought to evidence relations between the Parisi and
the Dodder people. Clarke and McCauley (2021) in
filmed recreations suggest dance partners would each
hook an index finger to the 'lunula' (half the bisected
ring) and take turns in leading their dance partner
until exhaustion or resistance would allow the lead to
swap. Forensic documentation of broken male index
fingers in human remains in Yorkshire from the period
has suggested to researchers evidence of a matriarchal
society.

No. 1123/29
2021.3-11   Amy McCauley / Gavin Clarke

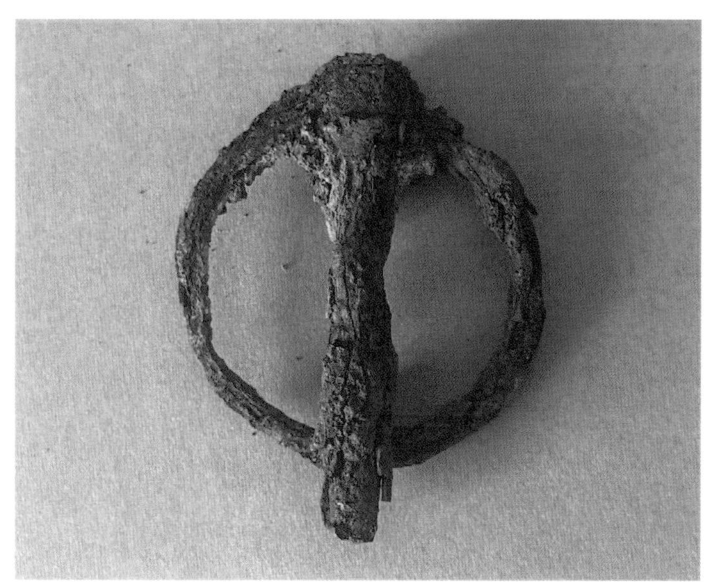

Mummified dragonfly

2500 BCE

The iridescent beauty of these miniature flying
dragons – which in highly oxygenated regions
developed wingspans of around 40 cm – inspired both
reverence and fear. Before mummification, their legs
and wings were pulled off, perhaps to prevent the
dragonflies from returning from the afterlife to haunt
the living. A. O. Shadcock has argued in *As Flies to
Wanton Boys* (2017) that the practice was a cathartic
ritual by which humans demonstrated to the gods
that they were not completely at their mercy, and that
cruelty could run both ways.

No. 1123/47
2021.3-29

Charles Boyle

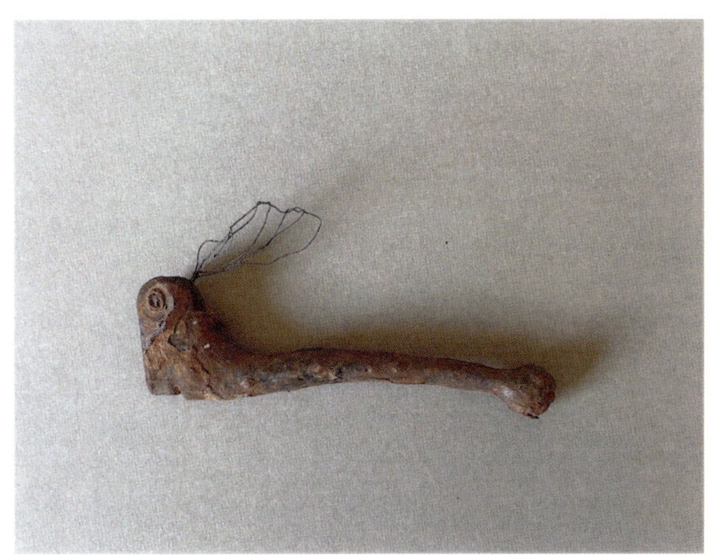

Ectoplasm Tube

In the late 19th century, the popularity of Spiritualism in Victorian society gave rise to a similar flourishing of fraudulent mediums who enriched themselves at the expense of the credulous. A common feature of these mediums' performances was the production of 'ectoplasm' (a term coined in 1894 by Charles Richet), supposed exteriorisations of spiritual energy by them through their orifices, which would then drape itself over non-physical presences, rendering them visible to corporeal eyes. Such mediums often employed compressed cheesecloth or gauze to give the effect of emanating ectoplasm that, as this exhibit attests, could be ejected from a cast iron tube inserted into the anus until stopped by the cross-bar, which was gripped tightly between the buttocks. Through the agency of a vigorous production of flatus, the gauze could then be made to inflate and float eerily behind the medium's back, whose ventriloquistic skills would enable it to apparently answer questions from séance attendees. This inflation was a difficult skill to master, and sometimes the ectoplasm tube could be blasted from the orifice with considerable force, shattering parlour windows as it was launched into smoky Victorian city skies – the rust on this example bears testimony to its final resting place in the Hampstead Road lock of Regent's Canal.

No. 1123/15
2021.3-18

Ian Duhig

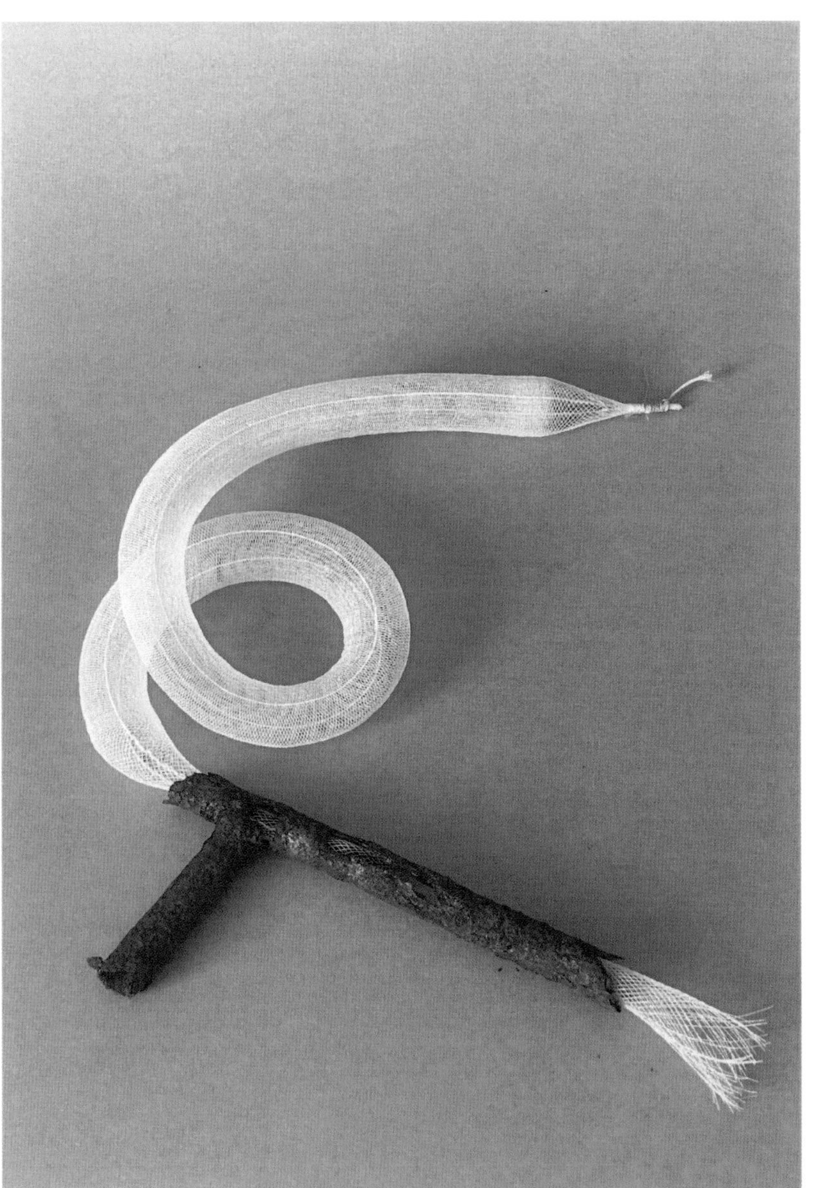

Industrial dream catcher

Early Anthropocene (?)

Two wheels thought to constitute the main elements
of an industrial-strength dream catcher. The wheels
are made from ferroalloys containing a significant
percentage of iron, which renders them both magnetic
and corrosive. These qualities were thought to
attract particularly bad and dystopian visions by
electrochemically bonding them to the iron molecules
of the dream catcher. This resulted in slow corrosion
and eventual decomposition of the object itself,
thereby physically destroying the previously intangible
power of nightmares.

The object is incomplete. There is evidence to
suggest that the two wheels may have been motorised,
spinning slowly in opposite directions in order to
safely disperse remaining unsequestered nightmare
molecules into the atmosphere.

No. 1123/45

2021.3-25

Natalia Zagórska-Thomas

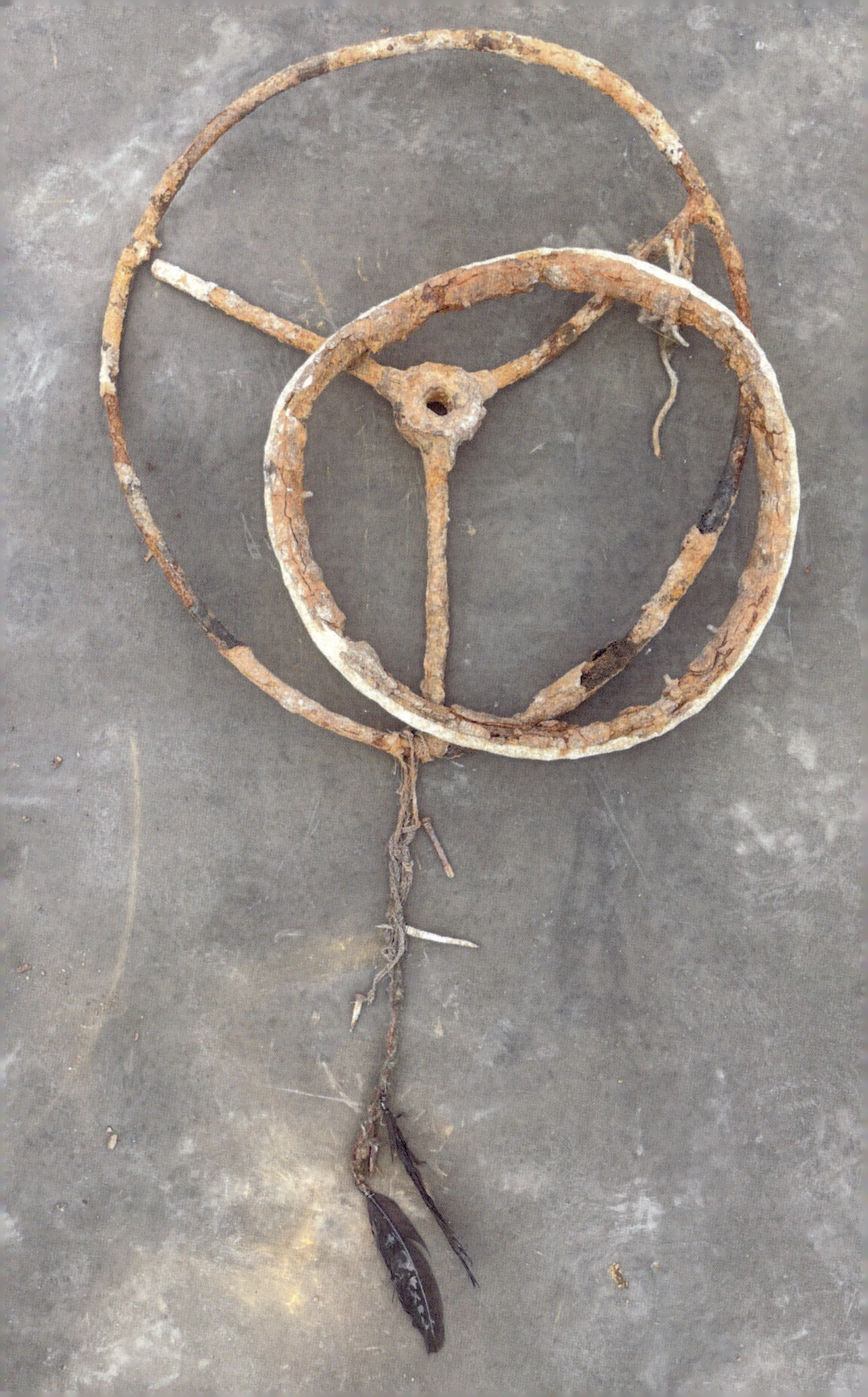

The Same Tether

This rusted metal object,
a tether's stake and base
where the farm dog is held,
looks like a scaly chicken leg

and its side-on view
is like the chicken's clawed foot
scratching the packed-down straw-strewn
earth of the farmyard.

Or I can imagine, more sinister,
this object bolted into the wooden wall
of an airless hold far below
the deck of a slaving ship,

and the wretched slave
tethered to it, who'll fortunately die
before being chained to an auction block
through the same tether.

No. 1123/39
2021.3-23   Ruth Fainlight

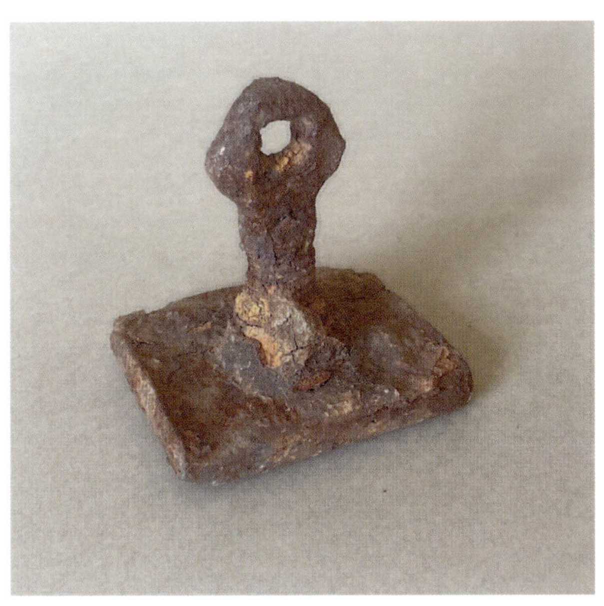

Iron curtain

Protohistorical fragment

Two pieces from a collection of fragments belonging
to the original curtain of iron, used as a symbolic divide
between warring tribes in protohistorical Britain.

Thought to have inspired the name for the political
and ideological boundary between Eastern and
Western Europe post WW2, as well as the physical
barrier erected in 1961 from steel and concrete which
divided East and West Berlin. The fall of the Berlin
Wall, as it was called, led to the reunification of
Germany and is often conflated in Western popular
imagination with the fall of the Iron Curtain.

No. 1123/01
2021.3-19   Natalia Zagórska-Thomas

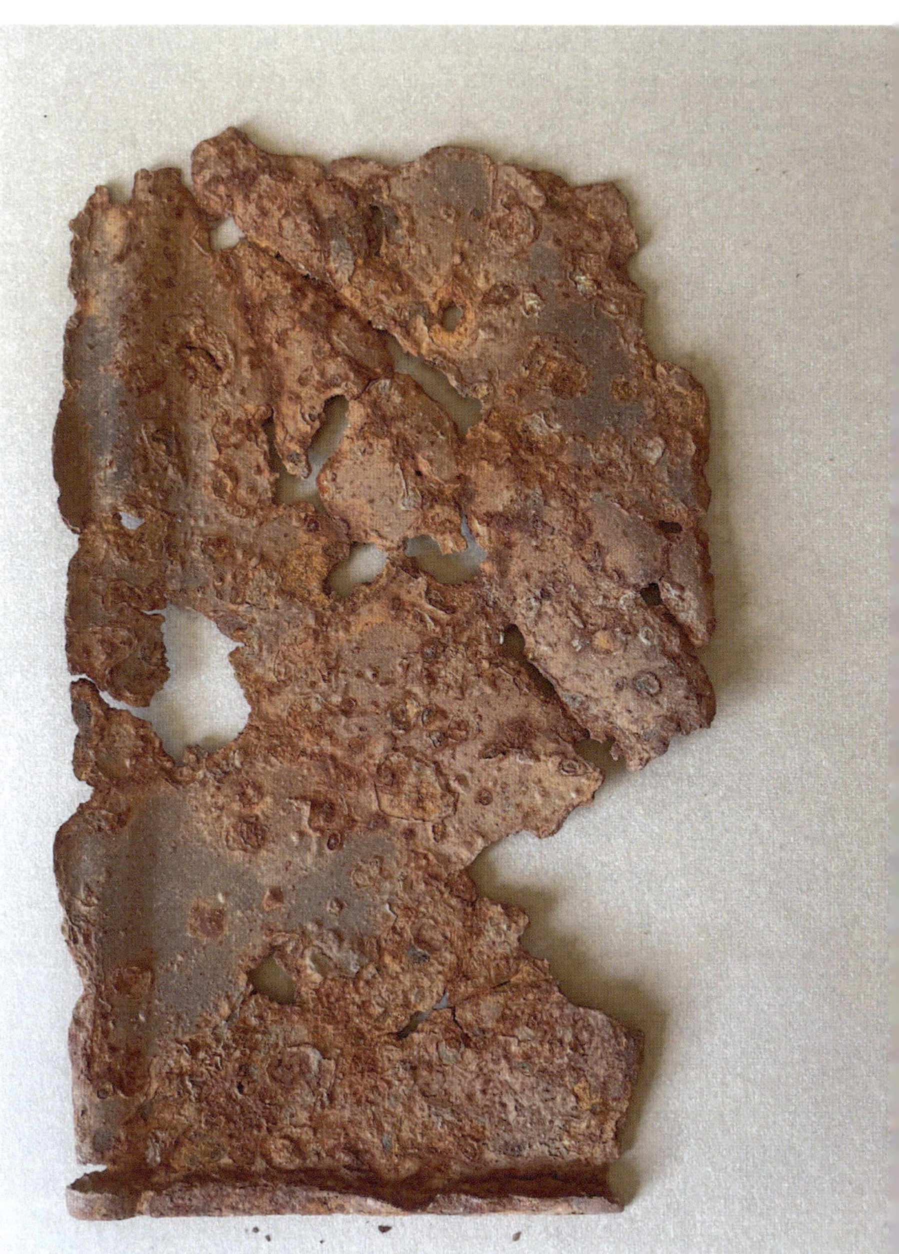

Pherometer

Late 20th century, USA

Developed in the 1960s by the R&D department of Argus & Wink, a California-based dating agency, as a tool for measuring your chances with a potential sexual partner. According to the intensity of the pheromones secreted by your companion and registered by the antenna, from one to a maximum score of the six red vials lit up. Well, I was there (the 1960s) and I can tell you that these things were as useless as those fish-shaped slivers of cellophane you used to get with your bill in Chinese restaurants which told you if you were passionate or fickle or dead. The only time even one of the vials glowed very faintly for me I was in the back of a pick-up with a very sick dog, hitching a ride to the vet. Or maybe I was doing it wrong?

No. 1123/08
2021.3-19   Charles Boyle

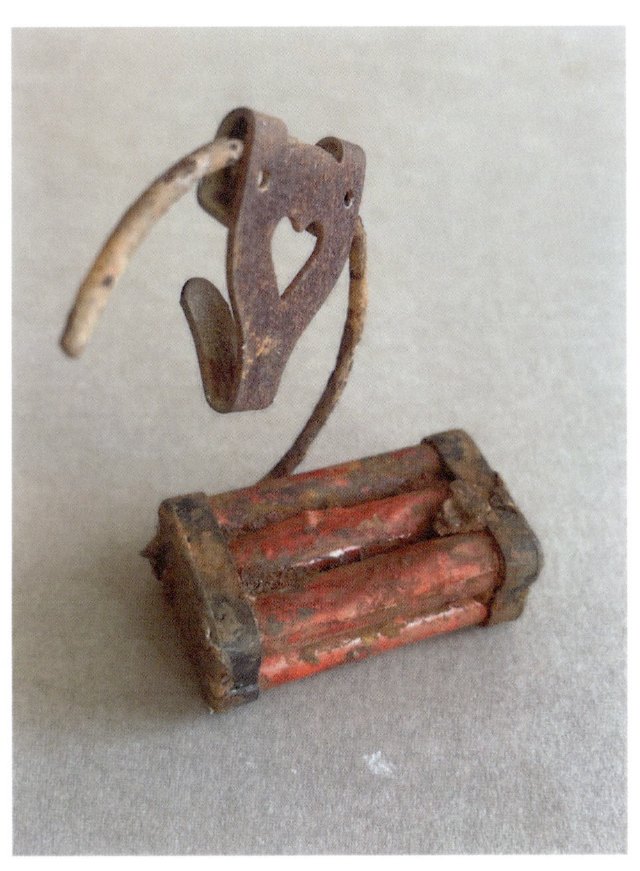

Fragment

Date unknown

Spots of cobalt blue, cinnabar and yellow ochre
indicate that this item was originally decorated,
probably with enamel (a chemical analysis has been
inconclusive). The three metal 'legs' are now of
different lengths, but it is surmised that they might
well have formed a tripod to support the central
circle of thick, primitive glass. As all the material is so
corroded and encrusted with mineral deposits from
the site where it was discovered, it was not possible to
determine whether the object was intended to be used
as a mirror or a sort of elementary magnifying glass.

No. 1123/55
2021.3-30   Ruth Fainlight

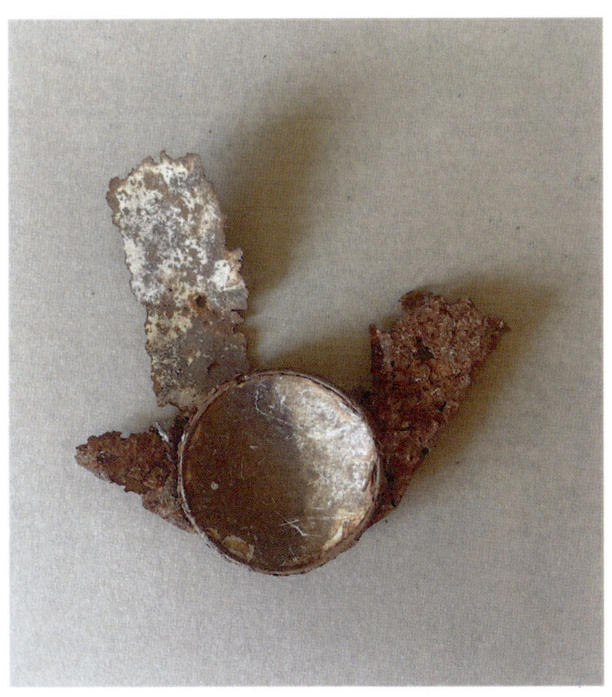

Bicycle seat
Steel, leather, date unknown

It's an Anglo-Saxon punishment collar,
the sort of thing they put round
your neck because you were a prisoner
or in the wrong place at the wrong time.
No bike rides for you, Wulfgar.
Just some garrotting around a fire.

No. 1123/42
2021.3-27   Julian Stannard

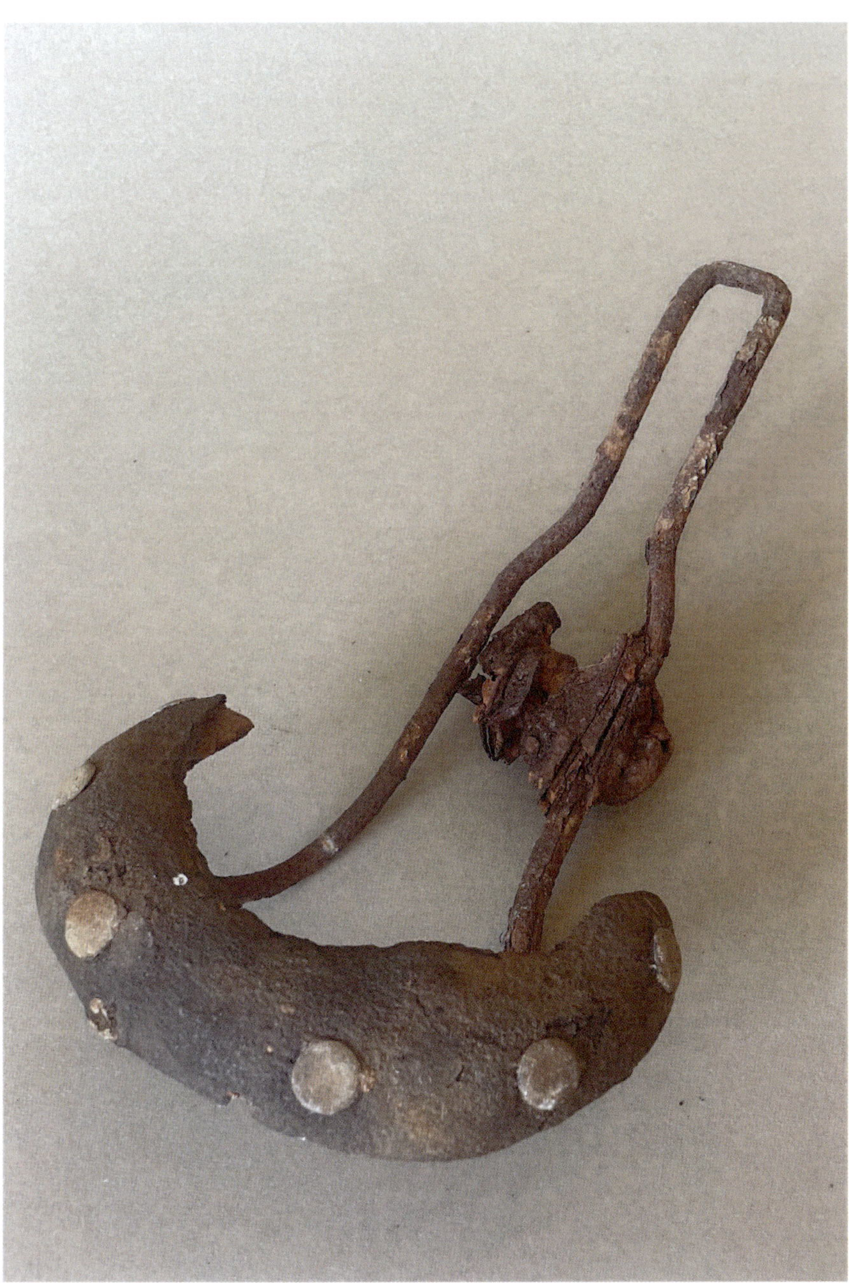

Wedding pipe (incomplete)

Origin: Scarborough, Yorkshire; *c.*200 BCE

Rare example of the marriage goods of the Dodder
people from Ireland discovered in the UK. Both stems
of this skilfully fashioned iron pipe originally curved
to allow the betrothed couple to face forwards and
to draw consecutively from the bowl while witnessed
by their gathered tribes. Traces of the mushroom
variety *Ptychopetalum*, an aphrodisiac, suggest the
ceremonial smoking of the pipe was intended to ensure
consummation of the union. Clarke and McCauley
(2021) suggest that bowls bearing the marks of the
respective tribes would have originally featured at
end of each stem. Once broken off at the start of the
ceremony, these bowls were likely exchanged by elders
as a permanent record of the union.

No. 1123/43

2021.3-10

Amy McCauley / Gavin Clarke

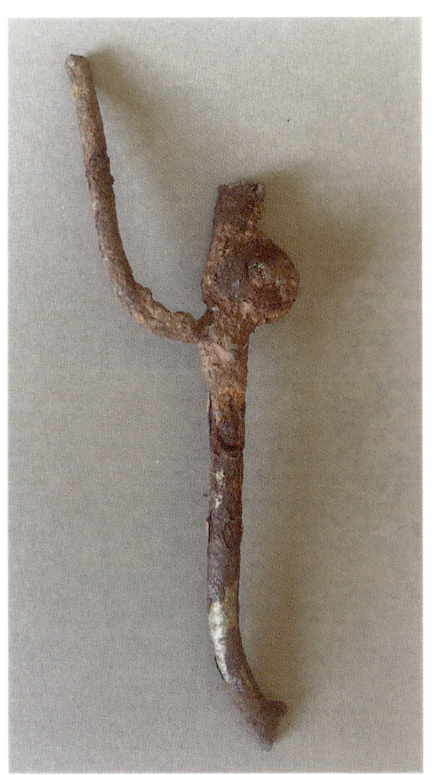

Teaselwangler

An instrument for removing a Conservative
minister's member from the mouth of a
pig or other similar mammal, as required by
circumstances.

No. 1123/19
2021.3-20
Mervyn Diese

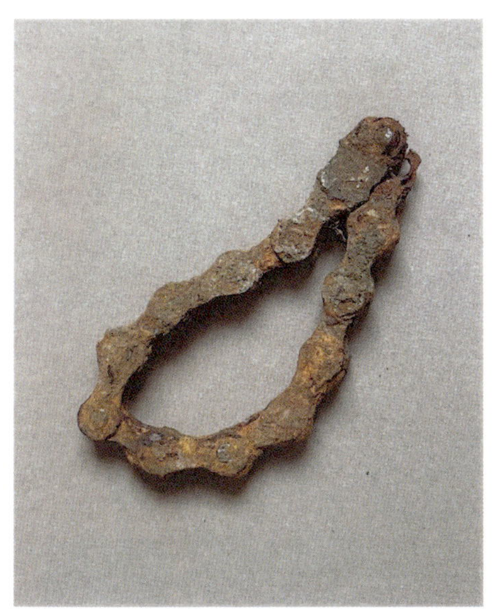

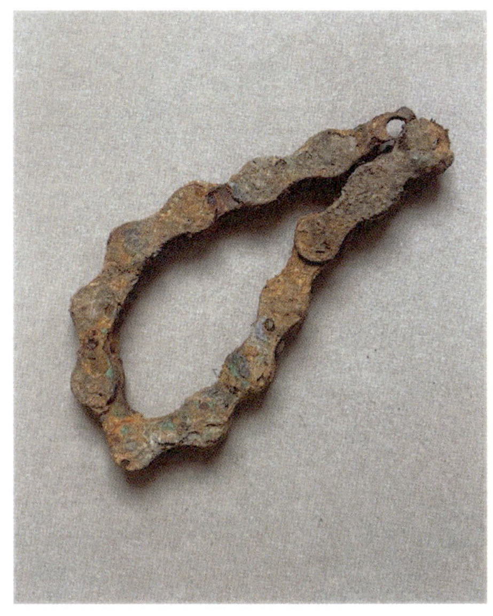

Deadline pin

This is an instrument of torture used on fairies who
have not learned to say no. The looped bit, known as
the 'swan song', is used for the initial bashing, and the
poky bit is obviously for more extreme cases. Fairies
are a mixed bunch, with cruelty rife amongst the more
bureaucratically minded and aged elites. They are
quick to punish what can be mistaken for waftiness in
certain sects. Many of the hardest-working fairies who
work closely with bugs to avert environmental collapse
have had run-ins with the deadline pin or other
jabber-type instruments. Usually the damage isn't
permanent, as there are tightly guarded spells that
reverse the effects of such torture and at the same
time strengthen the no-saying capacity. True fairies
like to keep away from metal and plastic, which have
corrosive effects on their magic. If you find a deadline
pin, wrap it in masking tape and dispose of it carefully.
Masking tape can often act as a buffer and neutraliser
between worlds.

No. 1123/15
2021.3-17

Sophie Herxheimer

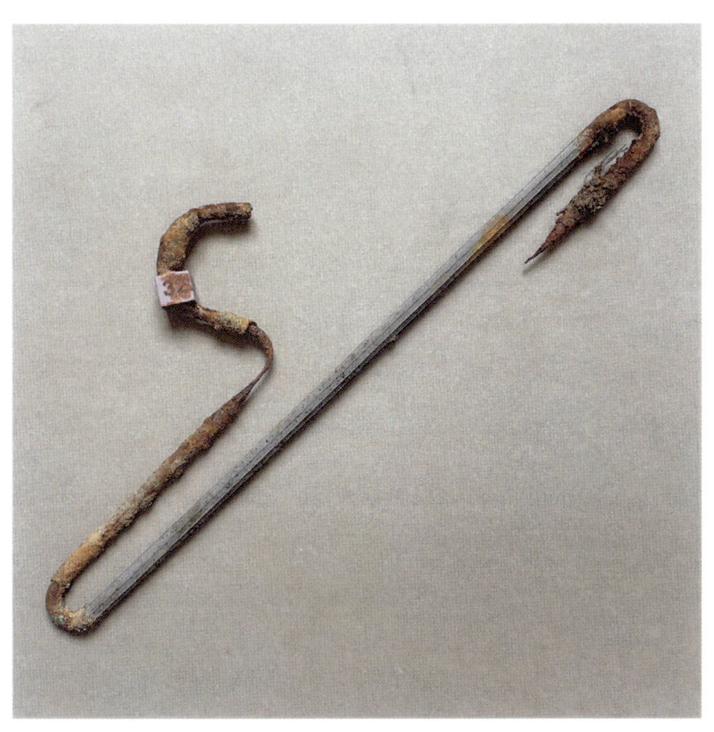

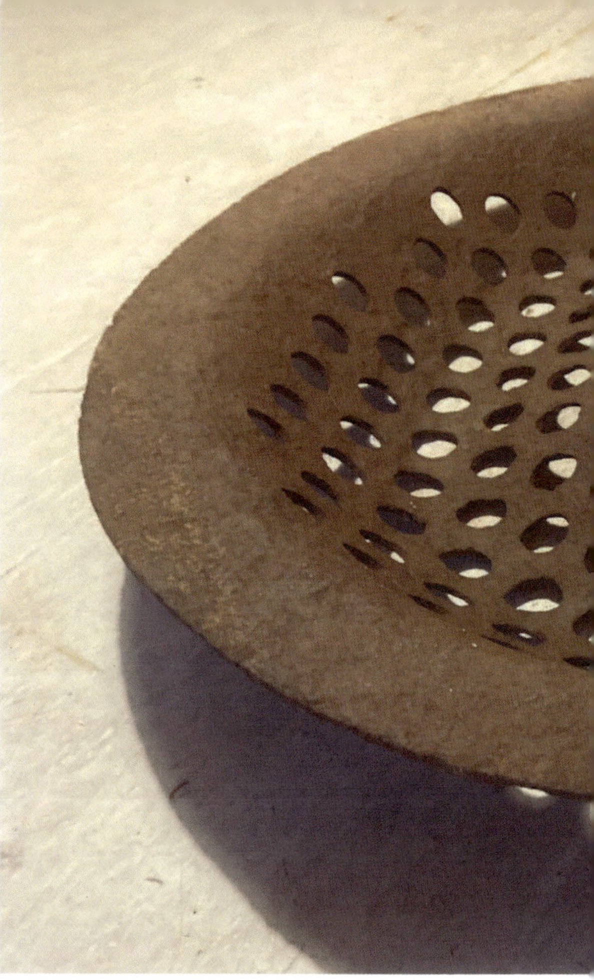

River strainer

8th century

Each summer during the reign of Hugo the Unwashed
(784–802) the Thames barrier was closed for a week and the
river was drained through a giant plughole at Gravesend.
The strainer was placed over the plughole to catch items of
value such as helmets, broadswords, bicycles and shopping
trolleys. A peace-loving king, Hugo commanded that all
objects caught in the strainer be melted down and recycled
as ploughshares; some historians have argued that this
practice left his kingdom unprepared to resist the Viking
invasions of the 9th century.

No. 1123/50

2021.3-20

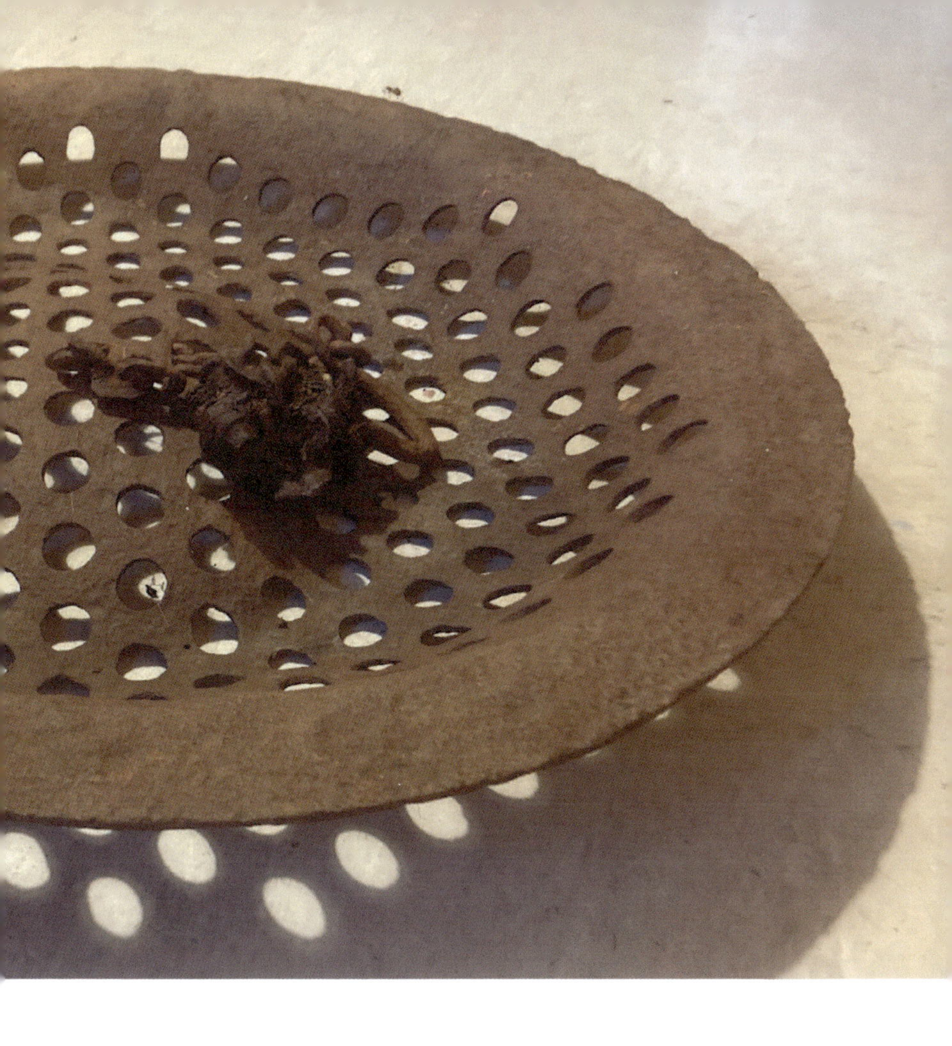

The Camden Venus

Estimated to be of early medieval date, this shapely and richly draped figurine is a fair match, though miniature, for the most sensual of Indian *yakshis* of a similar date, or even the Willendorf Venus, its most ancient precursor. Such English versions are virtually unknown and this one is certainly more beautiful and sensuous, despite its erosion, than the one or two other examples previously unearthed. The hand, drawn across the partially covered face, the delicate belly button and waist, the natural breasts and the rich folds of the glorious gamboge drape trimmed with Egyptian blue distinguish this find. Thought to be a figure held in the pocket to give men courage, its sensual form is so subtle as to suggest that it was probably made by a female rather than a male. Despite thermo-illuminescent tests, further researches as to its true provenance are ongoing because the use of gamboge as a colorant was previously thought to be unknown in Europe until the early 17th century. It is possible that, in fact, it is a very early import from the Indian subcontinent, Camden Town having long been a place for trading artefacts. It may also explain the atypically refined sensual abundance contained within its form.

No. 1123/06
2021.3-30b   Helen Wilks

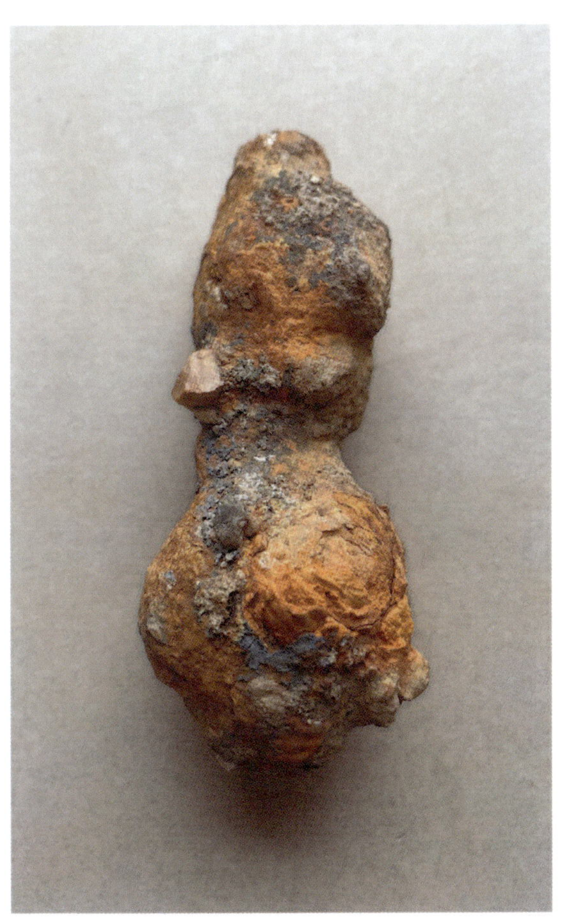

Bio-technological spine column

Date unknown

Partial, speculative reconstruction of a spinal column
from a collection of ferrous vertebrae excavated
together at the Regent's Canal site, London. The spine
belongs to an unknown species of which there appears
to be no record of any kind, in any human language. It
is unclear whether the creature had become extinct
or the vertebrae form a remnant of an aborted
bio-technological experiment. The spine is part of
an ongoing world-wide study into OOPS (Obscure
Objects of Perplexing Structure) funded with the
generous support of the Notional Heritage Trust.

No. 1123/01
2021.3-19   Natalia Zagórska-Thomas

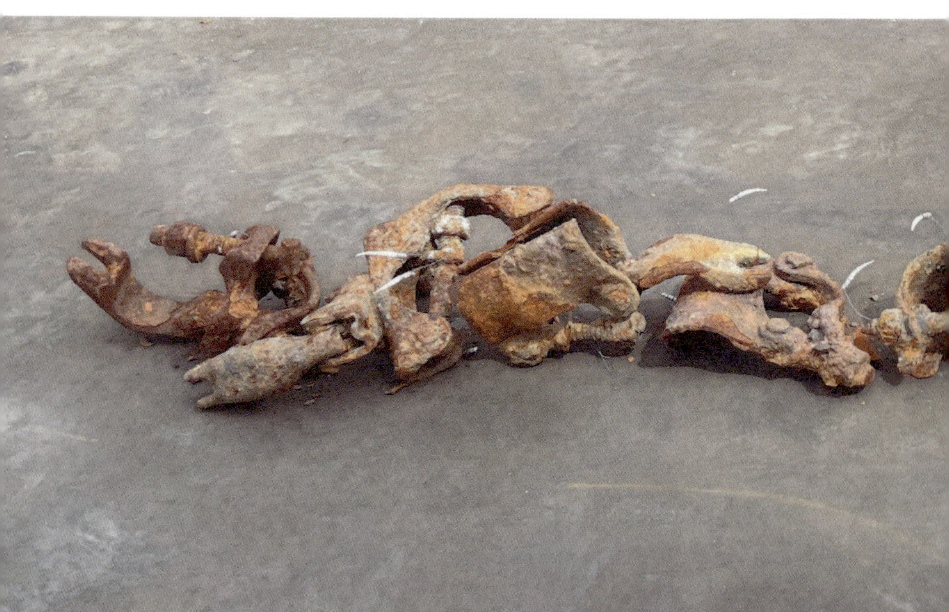

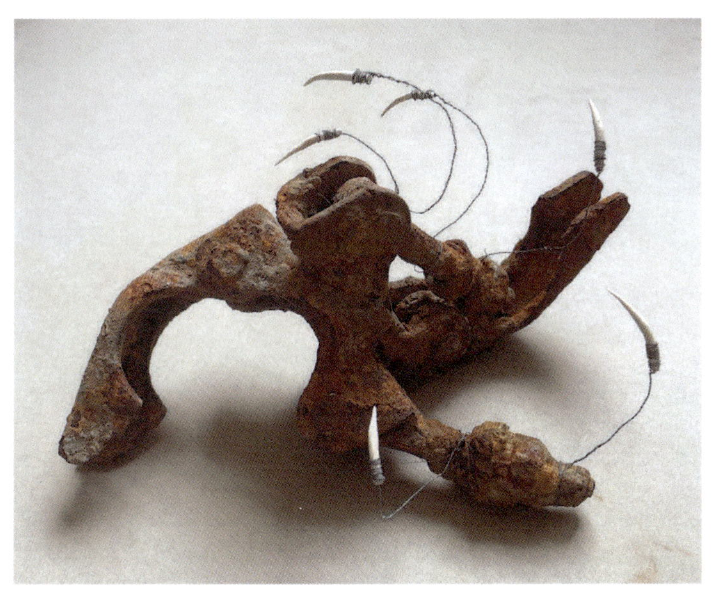

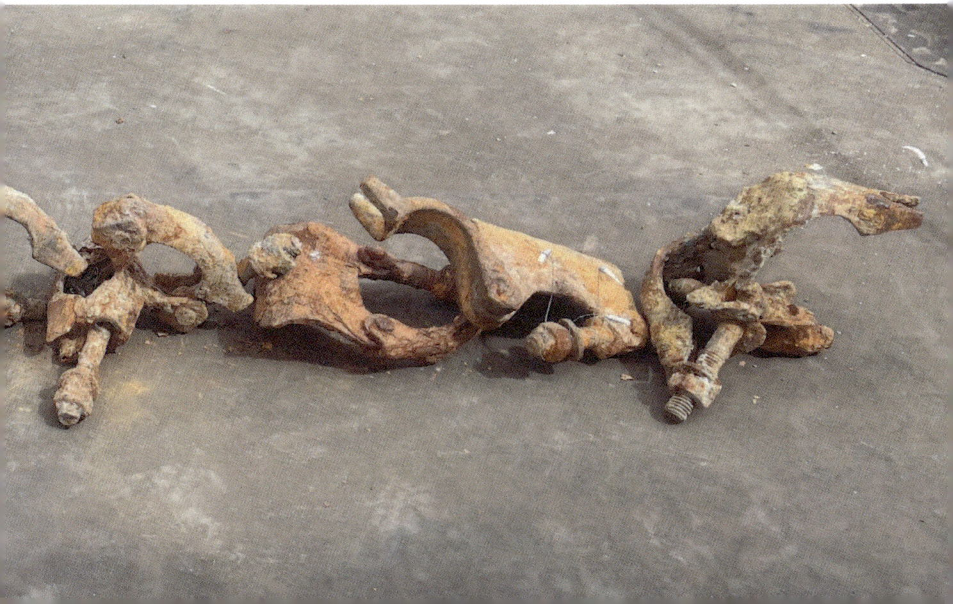

Two holes

Iron, Late Industrial

Talismanic representations of the void, thought to
have been kept by their owners as charms against
either oblivion or forgetfulness. Two of many millions
of examples fashioned from rusted metal in the Late
Industrial Period.

No. 1123/80
2021.3-12 C
Christoher Reid

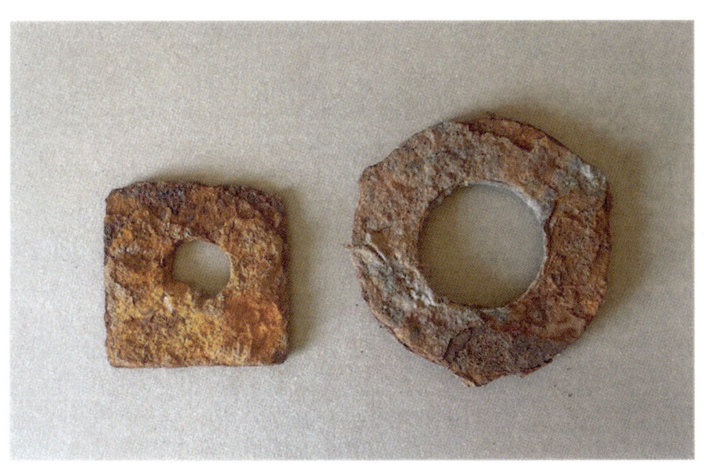

Iron recorders

German, mid-20th century

At the suggestion of Crispin Leotard, in the
*Darmstadt Akademie zur Integration Musikalischer
Traditionen*, the Moeck workshop produced several
metal instruments in the late 1950s. Leotard
wanted 'new' flutes and whistles, inspired by the
exploratory principles of the Darmstadt School, to
supplement existing instrumentation in his ensemble,
Contrabande. Hermann Moeck supervised the design
phase but after disagreements with Leotard passed
on responsibility for construction to his cousin, Dieter,
who worked for the local gas board.

Estate of C. Leotard in the DAIMT

No. 1123/44
2021.3-28   Will Eaves

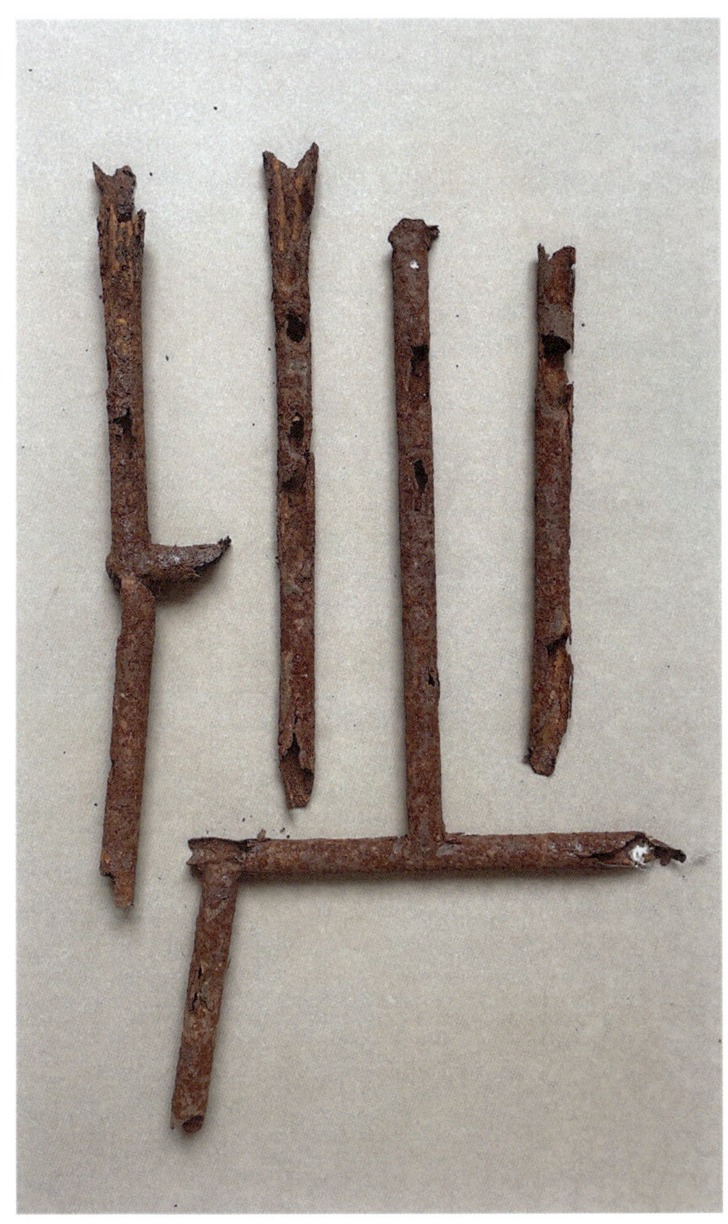

Mirror of Misery

20th century

One of many Mirrors of Misery dispensed by Caroline
N., who lived on Prince of Wales Road and worked
in the occult section of Camden's 'Compendium'
bookshop during the 1970s. Treated by locals with
distrust and fear, she dabbled in spells and had a
sideline in manifesting calamities to order with the aid
of small motorcycle mirrors. Once procured, the mirror
was used to to catch the reflection of the unfortunate
subject of the curse and was then immediately
wrapped up and returned to Caroline. Due to lack of
eye witnesses the final stage of the ritual is not known,
but many broken examples of such mirrors can still be
found at the bottom of the canal.

No. 1123/13
2021.3-20   Andrzej Maria Borkowski

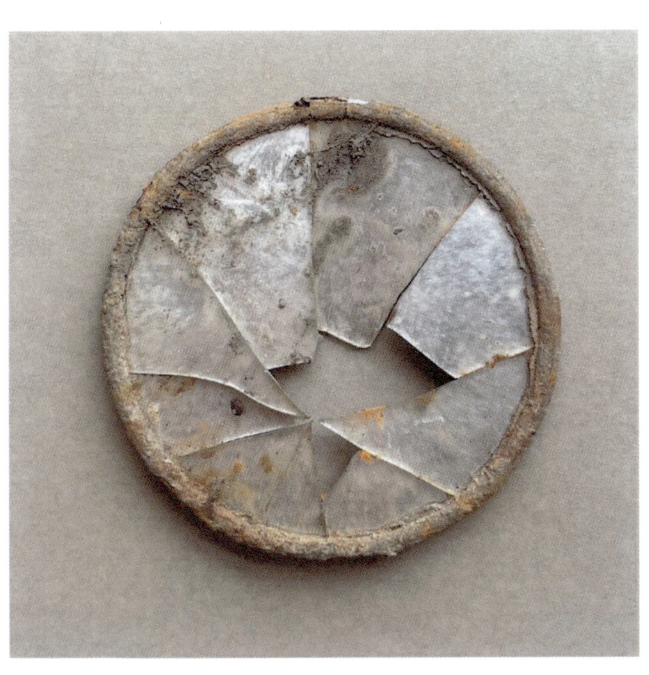

Christopher Reid

On Expurgamento

First printed in the catalogue accompanying *Ex Purgamento*, an exhibition of work by Natalia Zagórska-Thomas at Brook Street Gallery, Hay on Wye, in 2011

Ex purgamento: Latin for 'out of the dirt'. Refuse, in other words. Riddance. What nobody wants and has been scoured away. This, however, is where Natalia Zagórska-Thomas finds her material and her inspiration. She understands the mute eloquence of things – of objects, oddments, tools, fabrics – and wants to make them speak, or speak again, in her work. They may, after passing through her hands, speak louder than she does. That is one of the mysteries of her practice.

Zagórska-Thomas grew up in Poland in the 1970s and '80s. An early influence was the generation of Polish artists who came to prominence after the Second World War: Tadeusz Kantor, Wladyslaw Hasior, Magdalena Abakanowicz, Alina Szapocznikow, Konstanty Balka, and others. Whatever their similarities and differences, their art shared the need for new, redemptive forms of expression after the cataclysm of war.

It was, in its strategies, an art of making do and mending. It incorporated the humblest of materials – the discarded, the broken, the generally unconsidered – to make something new and vital.

Tensions and ambiguities prevailed. There was no doubting the seriousness of the enterprise, and yet a down-to-earth humour and knockabout theatricality were often part of it. Such objects as found themselves put to this roughly improvised, new use – a bucket, say, or a bicycle wheel – occupied a midway position, simultaneously declaring and denying their prosaic origins. So the detritus of material culture was made to provide visual metaphors for the immediate human condition: buckets and bicycle wheels seemingly caught in a struggle to remain true to their own natures, while at the same time evolving, elevating themselves above their decrepit and limiting physical state in the effort to convey larger meanings.

After working as an artist for several years, Zagórska-Thomas trained as a conservator specialising in historic textiles. Working as a conservator requires close attention to both the physical and the cultural essence of each object, whose physical condition will yield forensic evidence of its unique history. The relationship can in some ways be compared to that of doctor and patient.

Unlike a human patient, however, an object has no value beyond the meaning we assign to it; nor can it choose how it should be treated. It must remain passive in the face of physical intervention, which, no matter how careful, can only serve either to confirm or to alter its meaning. Yet many objects that a conservator handles have spent a relatively short time being either used for their intended purpose, at the beginning of their lives, or collected as cultural artefacts. Some have been hidden for hundreds, or even thousands, of years, in attics, in burial sites, embedded in earth or sunk deep beneath the sea. It is then that, safe from human interference, they undergo their greatest metamorphosis. They change shape, colour, texture, even chemical composition. Then sometimes, after this period of relative autonomy, they emerge, as if blinking, into a human culture totally foreign to the one they left behind.

What if such objects were not just passive recipients of our manipulation? What if they had identities, desires and ambitions of their own? In other words, what if, instead of merely reflecting humanity, they had the power to interpret and influence it? These are questions that Zagórska-Thomas asks through her art.

And the process that she hypothesises is something like this . . .

Let's assume that certain objects have outlived their usefulness. Through long contact with human beings, they have assimilated some of the symbolism placed upon them, then used it as a starting-point for their own pursuit of autonomous identity. Because they are not considered – by humans – valuable enough to be collected for themselves, they are engaged in a fight for survival. Taking such snippets of human experience as they have picked up from literature, visual art and music, they adapt them to create new meaning for themselves, one which will justify the value of their existence, not just to us, but to themselves as well.

Tadeusz Kantor said, 'A object exists between the rubbish heap and eternity.' It is in that space, suspended between destruction and immortality, that Zagórska-Thomas's objects fight with her for control of their own destiny.

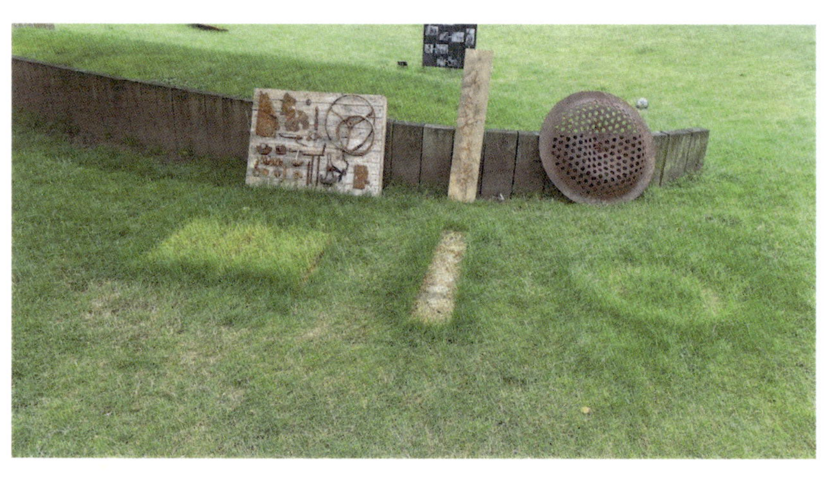

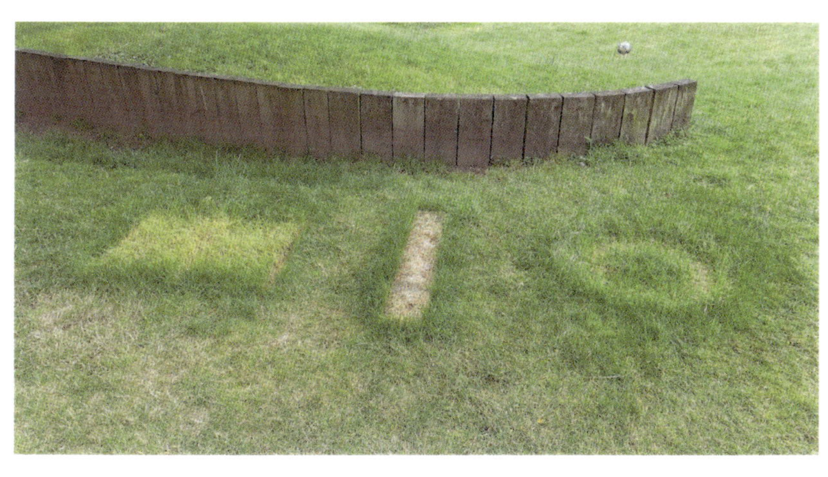